FROM BAGHDAD TO AMERICA

Life Lessons from a Dog Named Lava

JAY KOPELMAN
Lieutenant Colonel, USMC
(Ret)

FOREWORD BY WAYNE PACELLE, PRESIDENT AND
CEO, HUMANE SOCIETY OF THE UNITED STATES

SKYHORSE PUBLISHING

Skyhorse Publishing books may be purchased in bulk at special
discounts for sales promotion, corporate gifts, fund raising, or
educational purposes. Special editions can also be created to
specifications. For details, contact Special Sales Department,
Skyhorse Publishing, 555 Eighth Avenue, Suite 903, New York,
NY 10018 or info@skyhorsepublishing.com.

www.skyhorsepublishing.com

10 9 8 7 6 5 4 3 2 1

Library of Congress Cataloging-in-Publication Data

Kopelman, Jay.
    From Baghdad to America : life lessons from a dog named
Lava / Jay
Kopelman ; foreword by Wayne Pacelle.
        p. cm.
ISBN 978-1-60239-264-9 (alk. paper)
1. Dogs–California–Anecdotes. 2. Dog owners–
California–Anecdotes. 3. Iraq War, 2003—Personal narratives,
American. 4. Kopelman, Jay. I. Title.
    SF426.2.K64 2008
956.7044'3092–dc22
[B]
                            2008011736

Printed in the United States of America

"Dogs are our link to paradise. They don't know evil or
jealousy or discontent. To sit with a dog on a hillside
on a glorious afternoon is to be back in Eden, where
doing nothing was not boring—it was peace."

—MILAN KUNDERA

CONTENTS

FOREWORD

I couldn't put down Jay Kopelman's first book, *From Baghdad with Love*, and when I received the manuscript for the book you're holding now, I couldn't wait to read it. I figured that where the other book left off, this one would pick up, with the story of Lava the dog living the good life with Jay in Southern California.

It does do that, of course, yet it does so much more. This is the story of what happened after Lava got to the United States. But it's also the story of what happened to Jay Kopelman after he came home, to marriage, fatherhood, and the many challenges of a return to civilian life.

I think Jay would be the first to admit that when he rescued a puppy in Iraq, he had no idea what a life-altering experience it would be. For the simple act of saving a dog has done more than just enrich Jay's life. It has truly changed him.

By telling the story of what he and his fellow Marines did to save Lava, Jay has done something wonderful for animals. By sharing the story of his own journey toward greater self-awareness, Jay has done his fellow service members and his country an even greater service. Honor, Courage, and Commitment are the watchwords of the Marine, and by Jay's account, Marines typically aren't the touchy-feely, emotionally open types. Yet this is truly a narrative of introspection, personal adjustment, and love. It centers on Jay, but critical to the story is his wife, his two children, Lava, his fellow service members, and his Marine Corps.

Jay took some heat for rescuing and trying to bring home a dog, but not from those of us at The Humane Society of the United States (HSUS). The HSUS counts numerous service members and their families among its supporters, and between 2003 and 2008, I wrote four letters to two American Secretaries of Defense (Donald Rumsfeld and Robert Gates) on animal welfare issues.

From the start of the conflict in Iraq, The HSUS fielded calls from military personnel trying to bring animals back home from the war zone, and from all kinds of people disturbed about the Department of Defense's General Order 1-A. GO-1A effectively forbids American soldiers and Marines in zones of conflict from taking action to rescue and care for animals in distress. It's not exactly popular with the troops, and we quickly learned that numerous Americans in the war zone, including base officers, were doing a lot to help animals, working their way around GO-1A, where and when they could.

We encouraged the Department of Defense to support our troops by letting them keep and care for animals they encountered, and to take a more effective and humane approach to animal control challenges in conflict zones. We spoke out against the confiscation and destruction of soldiers' pets by military authorities and contractors. We even offered to help the Pentagon devise a plan for bringing mascots and pets to the United States for all qualified personnel, one animal per person, in an orderly fashion, with shots provided and a forever home guarantee.

We also heard from citizens angry about videotaped incidents of apparent cruelty by American service members, and we tried to persuade America's military leaders to discourage those (fortunately still rare) incidents of cruelty to animals by Americans in uniform. The HSUS called for revisions in the Uniform Code of Military Justice to make cruelty punishable under military law, just as it is under the law of any state.

An explicit prohibition would be a reasonable step, easily taken, and the clearest signal that there is zero tolerance for animal cruelty in the American military. In my letter to Secretary Gates, I wrote, "We recognize that such incidents are not typical of the fine men and women who defend and protect our nation in both peace and wartime. From our perspective, that's all the more reason for decisive action to identify and address wrongdoing by those few whose misconduct reflects poorly upon the rest."

We're still waiting for answers and positive response to these matters, but one thing is sure: Jay and Lava, and others like them, have put a face on these issues and it will be all the more difficult for our military leadership to overlook such concerns in the future.

In this book, Jay and Lava put a face on another important issue—one that concerns every returning veteran and one that should concern us all: the effects of stress, depression, detachment, and other negative emotions resulting from combat stress and trauma. Not every service member came home with a dog, but quite a number of those who have served in the defense of our nation came home to the challenge of post-traumatic stress disorder (PTSD) and related concerns. Jay addresses this issue with courage and sensitivity, and that's why *From Baghdad to America* has broad-reaching implications that go beyond its basic story of dog rescue.

Thus, to Jay's many heroic qualities can be added his openness about the struggle that he and others now face in confronting the complexities of life after combat. And to Lava's many designations—orphan, survivor, mascot, international traveler, playmate, and symbol—we can add another: therapy dog. I admire them both, and you will too.

Wayne Pacelle, President and CEO of
The Humane Society of the United States
April 2, 2008

For more than a half-century, The HSUS has been fighting for the protection of all animals, through advocacy, education, and hands-on programs. Celebrating animals and confronting cruelty, find HSUS on the web at www.humanesociety.org.

SPRING 2005, LA JOLLA, CALIFORNIA

"My dogs forgive anger in me, the arrogance in me, the brute in me. They forgive everything I do before I forgive myself."
—GUY DE LA VALDENE

You've probably guessed, judging by the cover of this book, that I have a special relationship with my dog. He's not just any dog. I brought him back from Iraq against all odds—and military regulations. I wrote that story already. *From Baghdad to America* is about what happened next, after I returned from Iraq. For starters, I broke up with my girlfriend of the time; I hardly recognized my former neighbors; I realized that nine out of ten people in my town were self-involved and over-entitled; and, worst of all by far, on one warm and sunny afternoon I somehow wound up watching Lava, my newly repatriated war mongrel, run into the street . . . straight into the path of an oncoming car.

Okay, so you're thinking, *What kind of asshole saves a dog from Iraq only to let him get killed by a car in San Diego?* And I really can't argue with you on that one. I mean, how in God's name do you reconcile something like this with everything you know to be right? You've survived the absolute worst conditions in the world, including rocket attacks, mortar attacks, and suicide bombs. You've made it safely from Iraq to Kuwait on a night flight to avoid the surface-to-air missiles. You come home to "America's Finest City," where you're surrounded by surf, mountains, and desert—not to mention your friends and family—you don't look before you cross the street one day, and *wham!* Just like that, it ends.

Well, it wasn't quite that bad, but it was pretty damn close for Lava.

I have him outside for a walk off-leash one afternoon. It's a beautiful Southern California spring day and we're enjoying the weather and each other, knowing we've been through hell and made it out the other side okay. I see a car coming down the street from the distance, and I know Lava doesn't notice it—or maybe it just doesn't register on him that here in America people drive cars too big for their skills at speeds approaching the sound barrier in otherwise peaceful residential neighborhoods.

So I approach him cautiously. First and foremost, I don't want to spook him. Lava is still a bit skittish; any quick movement in his direction sends him scampering for presumed safety, and he's just a few feet from the road. But as I get closer, predictably, he bolts. And the driver of the car—I know she sees us, or at least sees me standing by the side of the road—doesn't even slow down.

Her being in a hurry is obviously more important than safety or common sense (she's easily going forty-five, fifty miles an hour).

At this point I know we're in trouble. Lava's making a run for it, and not toward the house. I know this as surely as I know my name and Social Security number. Lava's going straight into the street, and there's nothing I can do to stop him. Time compresses so hard that for one brief moment, it stops.

Then it happens. Brakes grind, tires squeal, smoke and the acrid smell of burned rubber are in the air. Then a spine-tingling yelp of fear and pain as thirty pounds of dog encounters six thousand pounds of automobile.

But Lava is still the fighter I always knew he was. He doesn't lie in the middle of the road wounded and whimpering. No, Lava gets up before I can take even two steps toward him, and runs at full speed for the house, all the while continuing to howl as though the screaming will somehow propel him even faster to safety and salvation. It's the most bloodcurdling, heartrending yelp I've ever heard in my life, and I've heard some sounds come out of wounded men that would make you vomit on the spot. I feel like I've been hit, too. Lava is sprinting on three legs faster than I can ever hope to run on my best day. All I can do is run after him—and it isn't difficult to track him because the blood trail is heavy, let me tell you. I run so fast my shoes fly off my feet. All I can think of is getting to Lava and finding him help.

I know he's hurt— hurt badly—and I have to get to him, to hold him, to tell him it's okay. It's difficult to really believe that when you're looking at your dog's leg and can see the bones and tendons through a shredded, gaping hole. And you know he was dragged

3

beneath the car because his belly and the surface of his tail have been de-furred by the pavement. How can I tell my six-month-old, terrified, wounded—not injured, *wounded*—puppy that everything is going to be okay? How would you explain that to your infant child, for example?

My whole world is shifting—it's as if there has been a seismic shift and the North Pole has become the South—and I'm powerless.

It's happening again.

I wrap Lava in a blanket, get him in the car, and get him to a vet as fast as possible. My mind is racing, taunting me: *You broke the rules to get Lava here, and you deserve this. It's some kind of sick karma coming down and you're gonna lose Lava because you broke those fucking rules and saved a fucking dog. Asshole!*

I've never felt such sadness, anger, desperation, and grief all at once. My best friend was just returned to me a few days ago. *He can't die here, like this.* And then we're at the hospital, and he's on the operating table, and the veterinary technicians are frantically working to start an IV drip, take X-rays, assess the damage. The damage I caused by my carelessness and neglect. The absolute worst is when they won't let you see what they're doing; you don't know what they're thinking while they're working on him . . . *you have no control over whether he lives or dies.*

I'm a complete wreck of a human being when John Van Zante finds me at the hospital. I'm thinking to myself, *John helped me bring Lava back from Baghdad and was there at O'Hare Airport the day Lava landed in the United States—and now he's going to be here to see him go.* I'm not even sure why I called him, except that I thought he might understand. He does his best to console me, telling me that it wasn't my fault and that it happens all the time. He lets me off the hook with the bullshit all of us run to when we don't know where else to turn: *There was nothing you could do.* Yeah, except not let it happen. I'm back and not even sure where back is, and now I may have lost the only valuable thing I got out of Iraq. *There was nothing you could do.* Here I thought I was home, but it turns out that you really can't go home again. *Nothing you could do.* Getting Lava out was the best and hardest thing I've ever done and now I've gone and fucked even that up.

CHAPTER ONE

IF YOU CAN SAVE YOUR DOG, YOU CAN SAVE YOURSELF

"War is an ugly thing, but not the ugliest of things. The decayed and degraded state of moral and patriotic feeling which thinks that nothing is worth war is much worse."
—JOHN STUART MILL

"**W**hy *a dog?*" I was asked this question a lot after my first book, *From Baghdad, With Love,* was published. Reporters wanted to know why I put so much time and energy into bringing a puppy back to the States from wartime Iraq. *Why the hell not?* I always responded in my mind. *What were you doing for the effort—besides criticizing the administration and the war? At least I saved something from that place.*

The obvious point of such a question was that I should have been spending my time focused on saving something bigger—say, the lives of the people of Iraq. Not that I didn't try, but war doesn't play out in black-and-white like that. Besides, Lava needed me—needed all of us involved in his rescue—and never hesitated to remind me of that. Consider: On some level, saving the life of my dog saved me—and all those he touched—psychologically and emotionally, and continues to do so.

That's Lava for you. My scruffy little pup rescued from certain death in a war that he did not choose to be a part of, Operation Iraqi Freedom, and specifically the battle of Fallujah in November 2004. If what you're about to read sounds similar to, but not exactly like, any previous version of Lava's discovery and rescue, it's because it's not exactly like the previous version you've heard. Remember that game called Telephone? You know, the one you play a few years after you've mastered Ring Around the Rosie but before you get to Spin the Bottle? Where you tell someone something, then they tell the next person, and so on until finally the story coming out the other end is nothing like the original. Wartime engenders this phenomenon fairly often, because when we're not fighting or training, we're talking, telling stories. So that's pretty much what happened when the Lava rescue story started zipping around not only Iraq, but the United States as well.

From Baghdad, With Love included what I thought was an accurate recounting of the "canine rescue mission," as related to me by a Marine who'd told me he was closely involved. He'd been with the Lava Dogs—1st Battalion, 3rd Marines—in Iraq while they were clearing a house that would later become the battalion's command post in Fallujah. The way he told it, they heard a noise that sounded like ticking and crept up on it, not sure what to expect. Turned out to be a puppy wagging his tail in an empty room. But then I heard from Forrest Baker, a former U.S. Marine corporal and also a Lava Dog. He wrote me after reading my book, and lo and behold, the story this time was just a tad different. I wasn't surprised, since in this version Lava played a far more active role in his rescue by making his presence known. The Marines didn't just hear the sound of a tail thumping; no, they heard something a lot more insistent as Lava forced his way into being saved with his insane signature bark.

In a nutshell: This tiny puppy, who'd somehow ended up trapped in a fifty-five-gallon barrel, was making enough noise in the middle of a firefight not only to be heard but to let everyone know the troops' position, too. Forrest risked life and limb to get the dog, then brought him back to the safety of the house that would serve as their home for over a month and a half. And Lava's, despite the fact that it was a clear violation of General Order 1-A, Prohibited Activities for U.S. Department of Defense Personnel Present Within the United States Central Command (USCENTCOM) AOR, Title 10, United States Code, Section 164(c) and the Uniform Code of Military Justice (UCMJ), Title 10, United States Code, Sections 801–940, which somewhere down the line stated in no uncertain terms that "adopting as pets or mascots, caring for, or feeding any type of domestic or wild animal" was 100% *prohibited*. As in, "No pet dog for you, Soldier." Why? Because "the high operational tempo combined with often hazardous duty faced by U.S. forces in the region makes it prudent to restrict certain activities in order to maintain good order and discipline and ensure readiness." Be that as it may, the Lava Dogs named their pup and fell in love.

★★★

In case you've forgotten, let me take you back in time to November 2004, when this occurred . . .

The war in Iraq is still relatively new and the American public still holds out hope that what's billed as a war against al-Qaeda and the terrorist insurgency, and a fight to create a free and democratic Iraq, can be won (by the way, *it can,* but no one from the Pentagon is calling to ask my advice). The insurgency has placed a stranglehold on the city of Fallujah, a bad-guy bastion in the dreaded Iraqi Sunni Triangle. U.S. forces, predominantly Marines and soldiers, are preparing to invade the city considered by many reporters to be the most dangerous place on earth. We're going to assault Fallujah and rid it of the "thugs, mugs, and murderers" holding it and its people hostage, according to I Marine Expeditionary Force (I MEF) commanding general John Sattler.

Now imagine your nineteen-year-old son or brother or husband fighting for his life in what is the worst urban combat the Marines have experienced since the battle of Hue City in Vietnam more than three decades ago. And here, amid all the carnage—the beheaded bodies and the bloated, rotting, and charred corpses of what were once human beings—a group of kids, in the middle of an intense firefight, find a quivering bundle of fur. He is hope and life; he is a reminder of all that is good, of their former lives, of innocence lost. Lava becomes a link to everything that was once normal for the young combatants. War is possibly the most unnatural state in which you can find yourself, and Lava will alleviate this pain for you every single day.

He's a feral mutt with a shepherd-y thing going on. All furry face and raccoon eyes and a tail that never stops moving even when he's scarfing down the tidbits you've offered him from your own meal. Squint hard enough and he looks just like the dog you left at home, the dog waiting for you to return. In short, when we first find him, Lava is a tiny case of nerves and bravado. Warm, fits easily on your lap, grateful for any bit of love he gets and quick to return it.

In case of nervous breakdown, just pet him or throw a stick and watch him go. In those precious few moments of pure unbounded "puppiness" (Is that a word? It is now.), you're suddenly removed from your surroundings, as though you're Captain Kirk or Mister Spock and you've been beamed aboard the *Enterprise* only seconds before you become so much space dust because a Klingon has just pulverized your mortal soul with his laser gun.

Being with Lava can whisk you to that place you remember from your childhood. Picture this: Your puppy, oblivious to everything except your howls of delight, chases you, nipping at your heels when he can manage not to trip over his own hugely disproportionate paws that still somehow propel him after you in a tireless game of Chase Or Be Chased. Lava reminds the Marines that there's a reason for being—for staying alive—even if it's just for a few more minutes in an interminable day filled with the interminable nightmares of war.

I ask them what they want to do with the dog, what they expect will happen to him. I explain to them (as if they need to hear this bullshit yet again from yet another uptight officer) that keeping him is against the rules and they shouldn't become too attached to the little troublemaker because in all likelihood he isn't long for this life. How dare I utter such blasphemy in the presence of these not-so-long-ago innocents? How can I not? These kids need a dose of reality, and damned if I'm not the one to give it to them.

The young devil dogs tell me—with complete sincerity and total naïveté—that they want Lava to go home with them. He'll live in Hawaii the rest of his days, chasing turtles and lizards or whatever fauna roam those volcanic islands we call paradise. They want him to sail with them on U.S. Navy ships to Okinawa and then fly with them to their base in Kaneohe Bay. *You gotta be shitting me!* There's about as much chance of this happening as there is of us actually winning the war in Iraq as planned by former Secretary of Defense Donald Rumsfeld and former CENTCOM Commander Tommy Franks. But all I say is "Okay" and walk away.

Who am I to rain on their parade? Is it really my job to ruin their dreams of Lava living in doggy nirvana? Is that too cynical? I prefer to be called a realist. Dogs are not pets in Iraq. They're not adopted and cared for and put to bed on cozy doggy cushions from L.L. Bean. They are used for protecting property and shepherding flocks. They don't sleep on the bed with the kids or curl up on the floor at your feet while you drink a beer and watch *SportsCenter*. In Fallujah, in the end, they survive on the remains of the dead, only to be shot by us when they supposedly become a threat to our safety—a threat because we'll begin to care, to feel again, to be attached to a living thing who might compromise our ability to function as the cold-blooded, efficient terrorist hunter-killers that we have all trained hard to become. That we *have* become.

Still. I awaken one morning to find my feet don't quite go all the way down to the bottom of my sleeping bag. *What the hell?* I've heard the stories and seen the supposedly unretouched photos of alien-like camel spiders, and am immediately convinced that my superiors—who've grown tired of telling me to get a haircut and to shave—have finally found a way to off me without leaving evidence. Think about it: death by camel spider? It can't be better planned. Then the thing moves. It moves some more, and is now crawling its way toward my face. I lie still and don't breathe. Maybe if I act dead it won't bother to kill me again. *Shit, here it comes.* It's nearly on my face. I'm gonna die right here in a sleeping bag in Fallujah. How inglorious. What, I can't go out in a mortar attack or be shot by a sniper like a real Marine?

As I lie there thinking of all the things I should have done in life, and quite a few that I shouldn't have, I realize that the creature has broken the surface of my sleeping bag and is now . . . licking me? The hell? It seems that in the middle of the night, Lava found a way to crawl into my bag looking for a warm spot to sleep. How he survived the noxious fumes both he and I produce from the MREs ("Meal, Ready-to-Eat": a full ration self-contained in a flexible packet) that are the only thing on the menu here—and the beef jerky that I eat all too willingly —is anyone's guess. But at this moment I achieve utter clarity in what I need to do: *Save Lava!* Like Forrest Gump running back into the jungle in Vietnam to save Bubba, I am struck with a clarity of purpose and mission, of what needs to be done. It *must* be done. Not just for the Marines, not just for me, not just for Lava. And not because it'll make me feel all warm and fuzzy about myself. I have to save him because it's the right thing to do.

Later that same day I talk to the Marines who've been Lava's primary caregivers. I tell them I've come to a decision about Lava and what we should do with him. They reiterate their desire to have him come to Hawaii, but I explain the impossibility of that. The presence of a dog on a ship from Kuwait to Okinawa will be difficult, at best, to keep secret; he won't exactly be a welcome passenger on the flight from Okinawa to Hawaii (will he sit on the XO's lap?); and Hawaii, lest anyone forget, has some of the strictest animal quarantine regulations in the world. Not to mention, how do you explain to U.S. Customs the presence of an undocumented, unvaccinated animal upon landing at Kaneohe Bay? Uh, sorry, Mister Customs Man, but we just had to save this dog from Iraq, and now he's our official mascot, so you can't confiscate and euthanize him. *Yeah, right.* So here's how it's gonna go, fellas.

And at this moment I make the most important promise I've ever made, to date, to anyone in my life. I promise the Marines that I'll find Lava a home in the United States. One where he can play in the park—one where insurgents aren't firing RPGs at him, IEDs aren't a way of life, and dogs don't have to survive on the corpses of dead enemy combatants. How I'll do this I have no idea, but I've just given a bunch of young kids—your kids—my word. And I'll be damned if I'm going back on it.

You see, as an officer of Marines, your word is your bond. You don't ever ask a Marine to do something you're not willing to do or haven't already done hundreds of times yourself; you lead from the front; and you always keep your word. (Are you colonels—you know who you are—who worry about getting that star on your collar more than taking care of your Marines listening?) If I can't do this one simple thing for these troops, how can I expect them to follow me into combat? How can I ask them to follow me through a doorway into a house that's suspected of being an insurgent hideout? Answer: I can't. I have to make good on my promise or my credibility is completely shot. For that reason as much as any other, I was committed to saving Lava.

He may be a dog and not a person, but in his own way Lava saved me and my fellow Marines more completely than any human being could have during those dark days. On many days he continues to save me from myself. So yeah, I brought him back. *Oo-rah.*

Dear Jay,

I didn't think twice when one of my Marine buddies contacted me one day and told me about a good book he heard about on a rescued dog from Baghdad. Since just about every platoon out there had adopted an animal of some sort, and we had never even made it to Baghdad, I figured the chance of it being Lava was slim to none. However, I was doing research for a book of my own and was trying to get my hands on anything about Iraq I could find so I decided to pick it up. Yet when I went down to the bookstore and saw the cover I knew immediately that he was our dog. I couldn't believe it!

   I brought it home and read it in one sitting and I was far more than impressed with your effort to bring him to the States. It is nothing less than heroic. The introduction and story of his rescue is not right, though. I know because I was the one who found him.

Forrest Baker visiting Lava in San Diego

   The day Lava encountered his first American was far from silent. Hearing a grenade pin drop among the sounds of incoming mortars, artillery, and random bursts of both enemy and our own machine-gun fire would have been impossible for even

16

the keenest ear. Nonetheless, as we gathered in the courtyard of our newly occupied operations center to go over maps, the plan of the day, and enjoy the morning's first cigarette, one of the headquarters captains said that he could hear a whining like a trapped animal or possibly a wounded insurgent. We looked through the razor wire and sandbags atop the courtyard wall and saw nothing moving in the large dirt clearing on the other side. It was a desolate and bare battlefield except for the few blown-up vehicles, a 55-gallon metal drum, and scattered shards of metal debris, but there was certainly a loud noise echoing from somewhere. It turned out to be the sound of a hungry five-week-old puppy lost and alone in that metal drum, the only shelter he could find from the most dangerous place in the world.

The same captain then ordered me, a corporal at the time and the only NCO available, to shut it up because it was giving away our position. Luckily there was no time for micromanagement and he left the "how" up to me. Ironically, as you can probably remember, a week after we found him the RCT issued an order to euthanize all animals in the city in order to control disease, since they had been feasting on their previous and long-deceased owners. That option, however, never crossed my mind. I had to go get it.

So I then gathered two of the junior Marines on the forward to cover me as I ran out into the clearing. With a tight grip on the stock of my rifle I sprinted out to the steel container that echoed his

cry for help and used it to take cover. I had no idea
if I was being observed and if so by which direction.
The large clearing was completely surrounded by
two-story buildings and I knew my cover wasn't very
effective, or if it would even stop a round at all,
so I quickly reached in to grab him but he scooted
deeper inside to avoid my grasp. In order to reach
him I had to let go of my rifle, something we have
been trained never to do, and crawled in grabbing him
with both hands. I got up and ran as fast as I could
the hundred and fifty feet back to the courtyard with
my rifle dangling from its three-point sling. As of
then I had never been so exposed to danger in my
life, but luckily not a shot was fired.

He was so tiny that he fit into the palm of my
single hand. He was likely just being weaned and
missed his mother, who was nowhere to be seen. With
his white, gray, and black coat he looked as if he
had been singed in a fire, which gave Sgt. Julius
Hawkins the idea of calling him Lava.

As a forward command element under the charge of
Lt. Col. Ramos aka "Colonel Rambos," our operation
load was heavy, yet during the 38 nights that we spent
in Fallujah we did have a few chances to play with the
little guy and watch him grow, just as if he was one
of ours back home. He reminded me so much of my dog
Shasta that in a way it brought me thousands of miles
back to the U.S., if only for a few moments, till the
sound of gunfire would snap me back into reality.

When we finally left the city and returned to Camp
Owens to sleep in our own cots I was so relieved to

get out of there that I had forgotten to check up on
Lava and make sure he had a place to stay. I wasn't
all that worried, though. In that long and bloody
month he had certainly become the most popular member
of our company and I knew someone was bound to find
him a good home. I just never imagined that he would
have made it all the way back here. For me reading
your book was simply not enough. I just had to see
him alive and well for myself. Thank you for having
me come down to San Diego to reunite with him. I
still have a hard time believing that I was the first
to rescue the only good thing to come out of that
hell of a place. Yeah and you did a pretty good
job too.

Semper Fi,

Forrest Baker

CHAPTER TWO

YOU HAVE TO ALMOST LOSE SOMETHING (TWICE) TO FIND IT

"The greatness of a nation and its moral progress can be judged by the way it treats its animals."
—MAHATMA GANDHI

I **got Lava here despite all the odds**. Look at all the military guys trying to bring home adopted dogs—several of them wrote letters to me describing their wartime buddies, and the Humane Society even has a campaign to get the Department of Defense to change its rules about this. The stirring call to action in the form of a letter to then-Secretary of Defence Donald Rumsfeld on behalf of their members, lays the issue out beautifully:

As you know, GO-1A prohibits conduct that compromises character and morale.

We consider it ironic that GO-1A includes a prohibition on the keeping of mascots and pets, because the bond between humans and animals does not compromise character or morale; rather, it enhances them. In our view, it is the policy of confiscating and destroying unit mascots and rescued animals who have become pets, via euthanasia or gunshot, that may undermine the spirit of our fighting men and women. The destruction of these animals betrays the humane instincts of the service members who rescued them.

While conceding that soldiers have a primary duty to focus on their war zone missions, I would like to point out that our soldiers form bonds with the animals they have rescued, and take comfort in their presence . . . Moreover, there is a strong relationship between a standard of compassionate care for animals and the development of a civil society. Our soldiers' good instincts may serve a broader purpose consistent with our national commitment to the building of healthy, democratic, and humane polities.[1]

There was no response.

Then again, I never got called to the carpet by my superiors and none of the hired dog killers got to Lava, so by any measure I consider myself lucky. Then there's the fact that Lava and I both managed to stay alive and healthy, with all our limbs and organs accounted for and functioning. That's a lot more than I can say for many of my fellow Marines and countless soldiers. But when Lava was hit by that Land Rover, it turned me even more upside down than the straightforward weirdness of being back in civvie skivvies.

Everything I'd been so sure of, everything I'd been so coldly certain about, was shot to hell. When it happened, all I could do was berate myself as harshly and completely as I'd done to the Iraqi soldiers I'd been sent to train. "How could I be so careless, so stupid?" I muttered over and over in the veterinary hospital in that zone of unreality. Somehow the verbal abuse made me feel better. Throwback to officer candidate school, maybe? I wanted to have my body and soul broken down again, emptied. To have any sense of humanity drilled out of me again. It would be a relief. That was my comfort zone, after all.

If I hadn't been old enough to know better—and hadn't been such a pansy—I would have put my hand through a window so I could feel Lava's physical pain on at least some level. As though that would take the pain from him just a little bit and put it on me. Why couldn't I go back in time? Why couldn't I alter events so that my walking Lava at that precise moment wouldn't coincide with an inattentive driver speeding down the street? Could I figure out a way to possibly go back—like when Superman reverses the rotation of the Earth—and prevent the confluence of Lava's walk and one of those ladies-who-lunch going who-knows-where at warp speed?

I survived some really horrible shit in a bombed-out city halfway around the world. Now you're telling me that a lady-who-lunches, driving a big-ass SUV, is going to stymie me, a lieutenant colonel in the United States Marine Corps? Can someone help me, please? Anyone?

I suppose the modern world of medicine came to my rescue, as it does for those who can afford it. Lava survived, but it wasn't cheap. After numerous surgical procedures to clean and sew up his leg wound, Lava has fully recovered—to the tune of roughly eight thousand dollars. I know you're thinking I deserved it, and I probably did. It's really not the money, you know. I'd gladly have spent every last dime I had if that's what it took to save Lava. It's the feeling of helplessness that rips your heart from your chest and stomps on it with golf spikes—the old metal ones, not the new molded plastic ones—reminding you of what a useless human being you are. In those first few days of uncertainty (or should I say the second or third round of first few days) at nearly losing Lava, I promised myself that he'd never know pain again.

If nothing else, I promised I'd always be there to take care of him and save him from himself, and from my stupidity. I'd just have to see it coming.

★★★

I honestly can't give you a blow-by-blow of Lava's first moments in California. I do remember that I couldn't make eye contact with him because I knew I'd break down. But I also remember that I couldn't *not* make eye contact with him because Lava well, Lava doesn't let me get away with ignoring him, or ignoring what he means to me. The Helen Woodward Animal Center helped me bring him back, and a trainer there named Graham Bloem helped with what they call the "intake—" checking his heart, blood pressure, temperature, and all that.

Apparently Lava was pretty difficult to pin down for his exam. Graham has worked quite a bit with Lava since that day, and he's told me more than once that Lava definitely recognized me. "I could see the look in his eyes: He knew. It was quite an experience being there."

I was going through major turmoil in my personal life when Lava finally arrived, and having my dog back in my arms was the best feeling I'd had since returning. I felt it again after the accident. When I picked him up after he was hit by that car, I knew I mattered to him. He took my emotion—love, caring, whatever you want to call it—and reflected it back to me, as if I were a good person. As if I deserved to be loved. Without that, I think I would have gone as crazy here as I did in Balad, or al Walid, or anywhere else I was in Iraq other than Fallujah or Baghdad, where being unable to control Lava's fate tortured me that much more since I was physically removed from the little guy.

Lava forgave me over and over. Even when I'd visit him in the hospital and take him out to play while he hobbled on three legs, the fourth in a cast, he was nothing but excited to see me. He never made me feel as though *Look what you did to me* was on his mind. There was none of the vindictiveness, shock, or anger you'd expect from a person. It was only pure joy.

Dogs are known for that. People call it unconditional love, though I'm not sure that's the term I'd use. I've never been what you'd call a hard-core dog person. I didn't grow up with dogs. I don't get all mushy when I see them. I didn't even like Lava too much when I first met him, beyond thinking that he knew I wasn't sure about him, and he kept giving me these *I've got your number* looks until I'd reach down and give him a shove. He didn't give up on me. *Unconditional* isn't right, though. It's more like he trusted me to do the right thing in a way I'd never felt before. His trust in me gave me a different sort of strength than I'd ever had. It was a feeling I needed desperately at the time. I was supposed to be instilling that same sort of trust in the Iraqi troops I was training, and it wasn't working too well. There was no shared trust or shared vision.

In 2004 there didn't seem to be the level of emotional or nationalistic investment by the Iraqi military you would expect to see from people who wanted to live in a free, democratic and secure society. I'd like to think that this seems to be changing, slowly but surely, but I'm not sure. With Lava, the commitment never wavered. He was fully vested in his rescue and delivery to a free, democratic, and secure society—Southern California.

Lava impressed me with his drive. He never cowered in the corner. In this way, he is like a Marine. The Marine Corps has served in every American armed conflict since the Revolutionary War—and we're usually the first ones in. He's got the loyalty part down pat, too. Our motto is *Semper Fidelis,* often shortened to *Semper Fi.* That's Latin for "always faithful," and it's supposed to signify the dedication and loyalty that Marines retain for "Corps and Country" even after leaving service. Lava has that in spades. If he'd been captured he would have followed the Code of Conduct without blinking an eye. Memorizing the code was part of the drill at Officer Candidates School—and later at SERE (Survival, Evasion, Resistance and Escape) School—and no Marine ever forgets it.

Article I: I am an American, fighting in the armed forces which guard my country and our way of life. I am prepared to give my life in their defense.

Article II: I will never surrender of my own free will. If in command I will never surrender the members of my command while they still have the means to resist.

Article III: If I am captured, I will continue to resist by all means available. I will make every effort to escape and aid others to escape. I will accept neither parole nor special favors from the enemy.

Article IV: If I become a prisoner of war, I will keep faith with my fellow prisoners. I will give no information nor take part in any action which might be harmful to my comrades. If I am senior, I will take command. If not, I will obey the lawful orders of those appointed over me and will back them up in every way.

Article V: When questioned, should I become a prisoner of war, I am required to give name, rank, service, number, and date of birth. I will evade answering further questions to the utmost of my ability. I will make no oral or written statements disloyal to my country and its allies or harmful to their cause.

Article VI: I will never forget that I am an American, responsible for my actions, and dedicated to the principles which made my country free. I will trust in my God and in the United States of America.[2]

Lava would protect me and my family to the death. He was the same way in Iraq with me and everyone who helped take care of him. Make no mistake, however. It hasn't been all sweetness and light. Having a dog is like having a child who's eternally two years old. Lava wants to get into everything, yet he's clueless about the dangers of his actions.

I should have seen that right from the start, right when we first began giving him a new life. We de-wormed and de-flea'd Lava with kerosene and chewing tobacco (I don't think these are accepted methods among the veterinary organizations, but they seemed to work). We fed him, gave him shelter and a warm, dry place to sleep.

Without us, fate would have dealt him the card of death, sooner rather than later. Perhaps that fifty-five-gallon drum he first called home would have been blown up by friendly fire. He might have served as a four-legged IED (improvised explosive device)—the remotely detonated 155mm shells that insurgents plant in light poles, overpasses, guardrails, animals, and any other spots they can be hidden to maximize indiscriminate life-ending damage—intended to rid the land of the invading forces of Satan (that would be us, the U.S. and coalition forces in Iraq). Had he not been used as cannon fodder by the insurgents, he might have starved to death. Or been killed any number of ways: a wayward rocket; a bullet from a contracted Department of Defense exterminator or even an officer, as described in one of the many letters I've received since writing *From Baghdad, With Love;* drowning by an overzealous rule-abiding Marine, soldier, or sailor; being crushed beneath the tread of an M1A1 Abrams tank. Now I had to add to the list: possible death by Land Rover.

That experience jolted me alive again. And when I heard the good news, that Lava would live to run again, it struck me as clearly as if the heavens had opened and sent down a messenger cloaked in golden light: Lava embodied the most important lessons he'd taught me. That I still had the ability to love. That love would find me. That life matters.

Dear Colonel Kopelman,

I bought your book and raced home to dig up old memories. Memories from '53 – '54 Korea. There were friendly and loving dogs wandering around.

We had our share of war dogs: Donut (the eldest) was named for the roll of wire we used so much of. Dammit (middle) was named so we could get away with swearing at him without the chaplain being offended. T.L. (youngest) was named for a tool wiremen used.

After chow, we would go out with our tin plates and make sure the scrapings went to them.

Dammit in a photograph sent to Corporal Roche, nicknamed "Red Dog" because he was a radio operator and a redhead

Not one had a leash, and during the day, if we were busy, they went wandering around, some in dangerous spots. Some got in trouble with landmines.

There wasn't a hell of a lot to write about so I told my family about Dammit when I wrote home. My mother and my sister used to send packages to him. At

Christmas, they'd be
full of dog bones—there
might have been a
Hershey bar for me.

I had to leave the
dogs behind when I
was rotated home,
but they had lots of
admirers.

Roche with Donut

Thomas Roche

Tom Roche

Corporal, First Marine Division

T.L., the youngest pup

CHAPTER THREE

DESERT-COLORED GLASSES

"The days and weeks after you return from overseas duty will be a *transition*. During this time, service members often describe a range of emotions from excitement and relief, to stress, tension, or concern. . . . You may also feel distant, uninterested, or be overly critical and impatient with others. These types of behaviors and feelings are normal combat stress reactions."
—NATIONAL CENTER FOR PTSD

One day shortly after I redeployed ("came home," in civilian-speak) in April 2005, probably right around the time Lava was hit by the Land Rover, it dawned on me that nothing was familiar anymore. The town I'd lived in for nearly twelve years, the people I'd hung out with, the woman I'd loved, all the things that I'd once known so well were . . . gone. There's no other way to describe it. You think that life at home stands still while you're in combat. That everyone sits around waiting for you and your fellow Marines to come back and pick up where you left off. Nope. Life goes on at home—people go to the mall, they go to work, babies are born, relatives and friends die. The cycle of life continues, and sometimes you wonder what it's all for. All the fighting and death, when the folks back home just go about their business every day as though nothing's happened. As though the attacks of 9/11 never happened. Thanksgiving and Christmas come and go, you've missed another nephew's birth, you celebrate your own birthday in a foreign country without friends and family for what seems like the umpteenth consecutive year. How can people just take their freedoms for granted?

I hear people comment that we somehow "needed" 9/11, that it served as a wake-up call to our country. I just don't see how that's happened. A wake-up call for what? What actions have most Americans taken as even a sign of indignation with those responsible for 9/11? Have they stopped driving their gas-guzzling SUVs that are entirely dependent on Saudi oil? After all, it was the Saudis—starting with Osama bin Laden—who were at the heart of the attacks that fateful Tuesday morning. But all that's happened here is finger pointing and accusatory debate. I know people are frightened, but they don't seem to do anything about it—except complain when they're delayed at the airport for security checks.

Driving home from the veterinary hospital, I searched in vain for landmarks. I'd been in the military—both the Navy and the Marine Corps—for most of my adult life (for nearly twenty years at this point), and I'd made deployments and even been to Iraq previously at the outset of the war on terror in March 2003. But there was something different about this tour in this war and my return from it.

Lava had come to live with me, so to some degree I may have been seeing things through his eyes. To him, the posh yards of La Jolla, California, were as filled with danger and uncertainty as those fields of rubble in Fallujah. This is going to sound weird, but when he went ape-shit at the sound of the UPS truck lumbering down our street, or howled at the top of his lungs when someone, anyone, came to the door, or even when he—get this—took a piss on a nice couple's picnic blanket for no apparent reason . . . I knew what he was feeling. I felt it, too. We were back; where exactly we'd arrived, however, wasn't clear.

If you asked me how I was doing, though, I would have said I was fine. A-okay. I'd done my job, I didn't regret a moment of it (still don't, by the way), and I was moving on. I'd served my country. I was even able to bring home my best friend. As my mother always says, "When Jay sets out to do something, he does it." But she didn't believe me when I said I was fine. Better than fine. I didn't need to talk about the war, or what I'd seen. In fact, I was so tight-lipped about everything that my mother thought I surely must be working for the CIA. Lava had been there, and when he and I were together, we could just be, without thinking. No questioning glances, no narrowed eyes, no knowing nods.

Simply put, I just wanted to be alone with my dog. I wanted to see the happiness in his eyes when I took him running. He has a way of trotting with his head held high, tail curled over his body, and ears back, as if he's proud of me and of being with me ... but also 100 percent ready to tear apart anyone who doesn't agree that his owner is the coolest kick-ass guy in the park. I wanted to make him laugh by clowning around. You know, Charles Darwin observed that humans and animals have similar physical reactions to emotions. So when I laughed out loud at Lava, I know he was doing the same at me. (He could also be found trembling in fear and anger.) We played a mean game of tug-of-war, Lava growling and holding on until I inevitably gave up. The dog is relentless in his energy. To know Lava is to love him—or hate him—depending on his mood and your thoughts about having your leg humped or foot gnawed. In either case, though, he inspires strong feelings.

Speaking of which, my feelings those first months back were pretty toxic.

I tried my best to blame other people for my anger. I was pissed, and I didn't hesitate to let everyone know it. They'd sat on their fat asses while I dodged bullets or skirted dead bodies on the streets. And now that I'd returned, they had the audacity to question my decision to bring Lava back with me. There were people who actually questioned my fitness as an officer and a Marine. No doubt they were the same assholes who sat around drinking cheap beer and watching reality TV. That's the stereotype, anyway. Ironically, the liberal wine-sipping antiwar types (viewers of *Fog of War,* rather than avid fans of *Cops*) were just as likely to misunderstand me and my actions. Maybe they couldn't comprehend that level of dedication or commitment to something—or someone—besides themselves.

After the *CBS Evening News* aired a piece about me and Lava, people with nothing better to do (why else would they bother?) sent comments to a CBS blog, some calling for my return to active duty so that I could go before a court-martial for my crime: violating a well-intentioned but ultimately misguided regulation. They said I was a disgrace to the corps and to the country. That hurt, particularly in light of Dick Cheney's—and others'—Vietnam deferments. Cheney was the biggest hawk in the administration, and no one questioned his authority. CBS has removed all the critical comments from its Web site, which I think is a shame. The insanity should be there for all to witness.

From a YouTube viewer (proves a point, I think): "u ppl need therapy for real . . . 100s of innocent ppl dying everyday in iraq and ur concerned about a fucking DOG??? ur a sick puppy who-ever spent so much time on this in a war torn human rights disaster!!!"

I was also subject to some personal attacks in online book reviews. Not critiques of my book, but personal attacks. Several readers suggested that the entire story of finding and rescuing Lava was contrived. As in, *made up.*

Check out this piece of brilliant literary analysis: "I came to conclusion that there was no dog, and dog kind of represents the concept of hope that after US departure from Iraq, Iraqi people can live in peace, and LT Colonel was a savior, and was trying to give hope to Iraqi people. It is kind of metaphor." Genius, don't you think?

I've been accused of many things, such as spending six months playing with a dog in the sand. Tell me: How many of these critics were there when the smelly fuckers we were fighting were shooting at me and trying to blow me up? What? *I can't hear you!* That's what I thought.

We Marines don't whine about our job. It's the most important one that exists. We protect America. We protect the underdog. And above all, we protect one another. So when a well-dressed woman at a party looks at me pityingly, it's all I can do not to draw on my inner Jack Nicholson—remember him as the Marine colonel in *A Few Good Men?*—and remind her that I do the protecting she and her friends are all afraid to do. That to me, honor and loyalty are more than just words, they are a way of life that I'm willing to risk with my own. I'm not alone in this—all the way back to Odysseus, warriors have had to grapple with civilians who simply don't understand combat, who don't appreciate what's going on during the day-to-day existence of a soldier at war. Then we return and find we're expected to pretend that listening to our neighbor complain about our uncut lawn is actually worth a minute of time.

★ ★ ★

How does this square with the realization that I *am* back? I'm not shipping out again as I've done so many times. I'm here to stay, and taking a gander at some of the bad news showering down on us returning troops, I could definitely be in trouble.

I'd like to blame the entitled trainer at the gym, or the barista with attitude at Starbucks, but I probably also need to reconcile these facts in my mind: Soldiers and Marines returning from Iraq and Afghanistan are more likely than the average person to abuse alcohol and drugs, get divorced, and commit suicide. Military health care officials report seeing a spectrum of psychological issues, and a Pentagon task force gives the following statistics: Nearly half of returning National Guard members, 38 percent of soldiers, and 31 percent of Marines report mental health problems.[3] That's a lot of pain. Within the suicide data, one age group stands out: vets aged twenty through twenty-four who served in the "war on terror." Their suicide rates are two to four times higher than found among civilians the same age.[4] Twenty-year-olds should not be committing suicide—they should be going to college, meeting new girlfriends or boyfriends, and looking forward to the rest of their lives.

One really compelling fact jumps out from another Department of Defense screening. Combatants all fill out Pre- and Post-Deployment Health Assessments (PDHAs) when we deploy and when we come home. We're then supposed to complete another (the PDHRA—can you guess?—"reassessment") three to six months later. I included copies of these forms in the back of this book. Returning troops reported problems with interpersonal relationships four times more often between the first and second assessments in 2005.[5]

You can add my name to the broken relationships board. I shouldn't be surprised, considering that in 2007 divorce among Army officers was up 78 percent from 2003, the year of the Iraq invasion, and more than 350 percent from 2000. The Army explains: "The stressors are extreme in the officer corps, especially when we're at war, and officers have an overwhelming responsibility to take care of their soldiers as well as the soldiers' families. There's a lot of responsibility on the leaders' shoulders, which, I can assure you, takes away from the home life."[6] Label me Exhibit A, over here in the corner.

When I left for my second tour in Iraq in September 2004, my then girlfriend, whom I'll call Jane Doe, lived in one of the most affluent communities on the West Coast (not La Jolla, though). It wasn't the first time we'd been apart for an extended period—I'd had a two-month deployment to Qatar at the end of 2003—but it would be the first separation during which we knew there was a strong likelihood I'd see combat. As you can imagine, the stress of that alone—not knowing whether I'd return—can signal the end of a relationship for many people. Jane and I managed to keep the dream alive throughout my tour, but it was the beginning of the end, as I can now see. Neither of us wanted me to go into combat with a breakup hanging over my head, and we certainly weren't going to acknowledge the possibility before I left.

It didn't take long for things to go very wrong when I got back. Maybe—okay, definitely—I just wasn't ready to sign on with her for life, or maybe—again, definitely—I just didn't feel entirely comfortable in the relationship anymore. I was different. Not a different person, per se, but I'd definitely developed a different point of view about what's important in life. My priorities had changed. I think I'd be worried if they hadn't, after my experience. I'd never planned on being a gung-ho, tough-guy Marine out to kill. Nor did I have any altruistic dreams of saving the planet from one evil empire or another.

Consider this passage from *Jarhead* by Anthony Swofford, who knew in his heart from the age of fourteen that he'd be a

Marine when he was old enough. After all, his father, uncle, and grandfather had all served.

> Finally my mother peeled away the backing and steam rose from my shirt and on the shirt the glorious Eagle, Globe, and Anchor pulsed like a heart. . . . I ripped the shirt off I'd been wearing and poured my body into the USMC shirt, and the heat from the icon warmed my chest and my chest grew and I had become one of them, the Marines! At the ripe age of fourteen I'd decided my destiny . . .

Now consider yours truly at fourteen. I no more knew what I wanted to do with my life than I knew how to perform neurosurgery while flying a rocketship. At fourteen all I could think about relative to growing chests was the girls in my class. I don't think I was even aware what the Marine Corps was. One of our neighbors, Mr. Woehleber, was in the air force reserve, but he was still a corporate executive with one of the conglomerates that dominated the Pittsburgh business community back in the day.

The simple truth is that I didn't know what I wanted to do with my life, so I thought I'd give the military a try. I was three years out of college, teaching high school and coaching high school football. I'd tried a few other jobs, too, but nothing seemed to click for me. Playing war wasn't among my favorite things to do as a child. I preferred games and competitions with a quantifiable outcome—and my mother didn't let me play with guns or take riflery at camp. (Okay, I did shoot those damn .22 rifles anyway without telling her. As a kid, it was too embarrassing *not* to when everyone else was doing it. I didn't understand then that it was okay to be different, or to stand for something.) I was a kid during the assassination of the Kennedy brothers, John and Bobby, and after Bobby's and Martin Luther King's assassinations, any kind of violence made my parents crazy. Which is kind of ironic when I think about it, because I still got my ass or face cracked when I screwed up. They were shocked when I decided to go into the military.

Initially I just wanted to fly airplanes. And it's not like flying airplanes was a lifelong dream of mine, either. I wasn't like those guys whose fathers had flown in Vietnam and grandfathers had flown in Korea or World War II. To them, completing the navy's flight training was some sort of rite of passage (I guess it's supposed to be this prestigious thing, but I'm more impressed by someone who can perform brain surgery). I even knew a few whose fathers were still on active duty, admirals or generals, and who felt they had to live up to the family tradition. Me—well, I thought it seemed like something cool to do for a while.

I made it through the navy's aviation officer candidate school (that *Officer and a Gentleman* crap) and naval flight school (including carrier qualifications). One thing led to another, and there I was in Iraq, training Iraqi soldiers and trying to stay alive. So there was a trajectory of sorts, a ladder I'd been climbing, and I'd just kept on going until I wasn't sure I wanted to be up there anymore.

All this added up to my feeling lost when I first came back. Maybe not so much lost as disoriented. I guess you could say things seemed out of place, and at parties, even with friends, I often felt like I didn't belong. People would ask thoughtless questions— "Did you kill anyone?" "Did you get shot?" Is that what happens when people watch too much *Survivor* and *American Idol* and not enough CNN or Fox News? They think that war is a reality show?

No wonder Lava was my best pal—he'd been there. He understood. Jane simply did not. A lot of returning veterans seem to wind up getting wasted 24/7. If you're drunk or high, you probably don't notice how much you no longer fit into the world at large. But I'm older, and I hope wiser, and instead of disappearing into a drug- or alcohol-induced haze I just became miserable to be around, constantly noting privilege and entitlement.

Jane's and her friends' reality was as hard for me to comprehend as the harsh reality that our government condoned killing dogs to keep us from befriending them. I had grown used to driving by angry, worn-out Iraqis nearly every day when I was there—old men, young kids, mothers, their heads and faces covered by the traditional *hijab,* whom we had to move from their homes in Fallujah into tents on the barren outskirts so we could "safely" bomb the area in the name of freedom. Hearing people complain about, well, anything now struck me as absurd. In retrospect, what did I expect? They honestly had no idea what it was like. The local news didn't divulge that sort of information, which left me feeling helpless, unable to do anything except make snide comments. I could only call these Americans weak and pitiable, which of course didn't go over too well with my girlfriend.

On the commute to your air-conditioned office here, you don't see the burned and charred corpses of what were once human beings piled in the bed of what was once a pickup truck. You don't drive over the headless remains of a bloated enemy fighter with your SUV, the tires spinning on the fat oozing out the neck cavity and into the street on your way to the supermarket or going to pick up your kids at soccer practice. The scent of burning excrement doesn't perfume every waking moment of your day. You don't walk to the shitter with fear in your heart. Sure, I want to be rich as much as the next guy, but I'm not sure anymore if I could do it without feeling something for the guy suffering down the street. Don't get me wrong—I'm no bleeding heart. But I think there's a difference when you've sacrificed—or seen sacrifice—at the level I have.

Most of these people, my former neighbors and friends, never gave any of it a second thought. They thought hardship meant the maid was late. I couldn't figure out why everyone wasn't falling down laughing at a dinner party one night when I joked around about killing terrorists. There must have been some discussion of kids or viniculture or some other equally arcane thing and I just kind of blurted out, "Yeah, it's easier to shoot terrorists than it is to raise teenagers. You have to actually talk to your kids." Just like that. All you could hear were the crickets in the trees for the next fifteen seconds as everyone thought of something to say that wouldn't make the situation somehow worse. Of course, it didn't help that most of them, Jane included, had teenage children. Deep down I think the fathers all wanted to agree with me, but were afraid of never getting another blow job—from their wives at least—if they made even one comment that didn't fit into the PC culture of children as little adults, meant to command the same respect that one Marine might show another.

I mean, honestly, my parents never negotiated bedtime—or anything else for that matter—with me. It wasn't a democracy growing up in my house, and the dictator wasn't exactly benevolent. Curfew was curfew, you sat up straight at the table, chewed with your mouth closed, called adults Mister or Missus So-and-so, and God help you if you were late, disobedient, or rude. Every person at the party sported looks of horror on their faces as though I'd suddenly sprouted horns or suffered some grotesquely disfiguring illness or disease. *Don't these people realize there are real problems in the world right now? Leaders are being assassinated, oil is over a hundred bucks a barrel, and we're on the verge of a recession, for Chrissake.*

The discussion then turned to the merits of a Château Lafite Rothschild over a Château Léoville Las Cases. I wanted to puke. I can't even pronounce that shit, much less care how many bottles of it someone has in the cellar. When I was a kid we kept the washer and dryer in the cellar. I guess my folks didn't care about their wine.

I didn't puke. I picked my nose instead.

My feeling of not belonging didn't disappear after we left the party, either. Jane and I fought in the car, in the kitchen, you name it. It was enough to drive a man back to the killing fields. Plenty of guys go back again and again because they can't hack the monotony of regular life.

I'll admit it: We who've made the military a career can be—brace yourselves—rigid, anal, uncompromising, demanding, distant, emotionally detached, and overbearing. I know you're shocked to hear this. Right? I mean, look at how I poured my heart out in the first book. I even admit to crying when I got news about Lava— *twice!* How can I possibly be talking about the same person? Allow me to get back on point here. And the point is this: The world looks different after you've experienced war. The rose-colored glasses of youth have been torn off your face, stomped down by combat boots, and ground into the desert sand. Deployments— especially multiple deployments to combat zones—wreak havoc on marriages, families, and individuals.

So what was the likelihood that my relationship would survive when I returned? That I could successfully rekindle a romance following six and a half months of trying not to get killed, fighting for my country when no one seemed to appreciate it?

Your everyday, run-of-the-mill citizens can't relate to having an RPG explode or heavy machine-gun rounds impact just inches away. How could they? It's eerie to look back and realize that at the time you almost didn't recognize how close you were to having your head ripped off your shoulders by a hail of bullets powerful enough to punch a six-inch hole through the trunk of your Humvee *after* it first went through the vehicle's quarter-inch-thick steel side. It's not until later, when the firefight is over and you've had time to assess your good fortune (better than the other guys' for sure), that you begin to think of all the bad stuff: no more surfing; weeping parents; who'll take care of Lava; closed-casket funeral, definitely closed casket. Taking this into consideration, I'd say the chances of me maintaining my relationship were slim to none, and slim had left town on a bullet train.

I know that is a cavalier answer to a serious question, and I don't want to make light of the situation. Still, if I'd had the ability to recognize what was happening, things might have worked out differently. Perhaps I'd have realized that my frequent anger and frustration—which I directed at everything and everyone except myself—were born of the feelings I was trying to suck up and not let others see. Having the advantage now of time and some self-reflection, I can see that I was a jerk, behaving more like a child than a responsible, mature adult. Intentionally? Maybe. Was it my fault? Yes and no. I could make the argument that I am just another statistic. (I've included some of the original studies; check them out yourself.)

But I'm supposed to be smarter than that—better than that. I've come to learn that you can't always control the fear, hurt, and anger by suppressing it. Trying to appear strong on the outside when inside you're hurting and conflicted isn't going to work. I recognized this in Lava, especially when the fear got too strong for him. He was terrified of the ocean. Absolutely, whole-body-shaking, refusing-to-move terrified. Did the waves crashing on the sand sound like bombs to him? Was the shifting sand underfoot a reminder of his previous feral and uncertain existence? I could see this in him, and even think about how I could help him function despite it, but I believed with the conviction of a zealot that none of my experiences had shaken me in the same way.

I don't exhibit the classic symptoms of post-traumatic stress disorder (PTSD). Lava does, as I'll spell out later, but I really don't. In fact, until I started writing this book, I didn't think I had any issues coming out of the war.

I've read the stories in *The New York Times,* and I think I'm doing better than most. Unlike Lance Corporal Walter Rollo Smith, I never found myself bawling on the rifle range after returning from Iraq. Unlike him, I didn't hold my girlfriend underwater until she was no longer breathing, leaving twin babies without a mother.

Like him, though, I saw similar things in Iraq: "I watched this kid's head get blown away, his brains splattering while his screams still echoed," Smith told a reporter. Like him, I wouldn't blame the war for everything: "I can't completely, honestly say that, yes, PTSD was the sole cause of what I did. . . . I don't want to use it as a crutch. I'd feel like I was copping out of something . . . [but] before I went to Iraq, there's no way I would have taken somebody else's life."[7] I wasn't driven to volunteer for dangerous, nearly suicidal missions like Specialist James Gregg, a National Guardsman whose job it was to stand guard at a checkpoint. Having Iraqi citizens come to him day after day, holding the bodies of their loved ones, dead or wounded, screaming that it was his fault, scrambled his mind. Soon after returning to South Dakota, Gregg put five bullets into a man who'd beaten him in a bar brawl over a girl.[8]

Can I give Lava the credit for keeping me from crossing that line? He couldn't stop me from ending a relationship (he was probably as happy as I was to break that one off, to be honest). But who am I to say? Maybe deep down I knew that I was having some trouble connecting with people, but I was unable—or unwilling—to acknowledge it and make the changes necessary to be a better person when I returned from Iraq for the last time. I guess in the ensuing months—after Lava and I had some time to ourselves—I was finally able to resolve some things with (and within) myself, making it possible for me to be a stronger, more self-assured person, wanting to be in a committed and loving relationship.

Yes, I've made mistakes in the past, but I believe things happen for a reason and that everything has a way of working out for the best. How do I maintain this belief with all the young kids who've been killed or wounded in the war? In any war? That somehow their deaths happened "for the best"? I don't know that I can answer that question, and it's something I struggle with from time to time.

I guess in this case maybe that's what I *need* to believe. So be it. Am I sorry for what happened in that relationship? I suppose on one level I am—at least for the way I behaved some of the time. Being rude, arrogant, belligerent; seeing the negative in everything; expecting the worst. But I am also eternally grateful. If not for the place Lava and I found ourselves after the relationship ended, we would not have discovered the loving embrace of the family we now have—the wonderful, loving, *perfect* family that Lava in fact found for us. My family is everything in the world to me, and I'd sooner die a thousand deaths than spend even one day, much less live my life, without them.

Dear Sir:

I read the story of
Jay Kopelman and
was taken back [to
my past] to hear
what he and others
did to get his dog,
Lava, back to the
States.

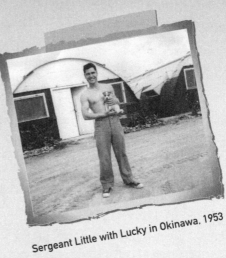

Sergeant Little with Lucky in Okinawa, 1953

I can relate to
what a person will
do for a dog. I was
a Marine on Okinawa,
Japan, back in late
1953 when I found my
pup. Dogs were scarce there and we had to guard him
with our lives.

Lucky enjoying his days at the base

The pup was loved
by all in my com-
pany. I went through
different channels
to get the dog back,
to no avail.

Needless to say, I had to leave the pup on the island. The other troops would adopt him and take care of him after I left.

Jay was one lucky guy.

P.S. The pup's name was Lucky.

Lucky trying his hand at driving

James J. Little

Sergeant, Third Marine Division, D Company

CHAPTER FOUR

LOVE WALKS IN, THANKS TO LAVA

"We long for an affection altogether ignorant of our faults. Heaven has accorded this to us in the uncritical canine attachment."

—GEORGE ELIOT

How can I credit my dog with finding my family for me? Let me count the ways. For one thing, his companionship during those tough first few months back let me open up enough to allow it. For another, he occasionally reminded me that both of us needed more in our lives than each other. And finally, he literally did find Pam for me. For us. It was in typical Lava fashion: He simply raced up to a gorgeous woman at the park whom I'd noticed on previous outings, homed in on her seven-year-old son, and dragged the boy to the ground as if he were another puppy. I didn't see this entire scenario unfold, but because my wife swears it did, I have to believe her. (I like to think it was a way for her to start a deeper conversation with me without being too obvious.) This is the way the op went down: One minute I was talking to another of the local dog owners, and the next, "Hey, your dog bit my son!" Panic struck. In La Jolla, the penalty for a dog bite is euthanasia for the offender, the owner, and all their kind.

I ran to them as fast as I could, expecting to see a gaping wound where Lava had sunk his fangs into this poor child's arm or leg and taken out a chunk of flesh. Instead, much to my relief, there was mostly dog saliva on the boy's wrist. In that moment of giddiness over my worst fears not being realized, I quickly regained my composure, put a look of deep concern on my face, and said, "Well, does your son have any diseases I should worry about?" Smooth, no? Man, I am Rico Suave, am I not? What woman could resist that line? That witticism? She should have been dropping her panties for me right then and there. Well, that's how I like to tell the story anyway—and some of my friends not-so-jokingly say I really believe it might have happened that way.

They have suggested at times that I was still in predator mode, a warrior hunting for his prey, lying in wait—the hunter-killer mode that I'd so easily fallen into in Iraq and that had become so much a part of me, both in body and soul. Not exactly flattering, but it's definitely something I've considered. Lava had worked hard on me to break this pattern and focus on the more important particulars of life such as playing with a stick, but I'd been a Marine for far longer than he'd been alive. In this case, however, I'll let the comments slide, as sometimes the ends justify the means. Which they absolutely have.

I do know that after I nearly pissed my pants with fear and concern over the alleged dog bite, I very sincerely asked if the boy was okay and checked him out thoroughly, making a mental note to myself to call my attorneys first thing in the morning—just in case. The beauty of all this, however, was that it put me in close proximity to a lovely woman and gave me the opening I'd been looking for. I sat down next to her and began what was probably our first real conversation, despite the nerves I was feeling.

Over the next few weeks, I'd see Pam at the park and we'd talk about the mundane and the interesting, though the courtship really wasn't going anywhere yet. Then, one Sunday morning—October 2, 2005, to be exact—I was at the park early with Lava. There was no one else around at that hour, and I couldn't help thinking about what a great day it was going to be and how it could only be more perfect if, during this period of calm, Pam just happened to show up alone with her dog so that I could really get down to business. And then, as though the angels had heard me, it happened. I saw Koda (Pam's dog) first as she rounded the corner, followed by Pam, wearing flip-flops; the white denim mini skirt with the frayed hem that I'd come to love because it showed off her lean, tan, muscular legs so very nicely; and her trademark Ironman (outrigger canoeing competition) sweatshirt that had allowed me my first opening when I inquired once if she did triathlons and if she'd actually done Ironman Hawaii.

She approached from the southwest, the sunlight glowing on her auburn hair, an aura literally surrounding her. She moved with the ease and grace of an athlete, at the same time exhibiting an almost feline quality (tiger or lioness) that allowed her to exude sensuality and sexuality in every step. My heart did backflips, my mouth went temporarily dry as I smiled like the village idiot and waved. She came over, sitting next to me on the wall while the dogs played. We mostly just watched them, but after several minutes of not talking—though the tension was palpable—I said, "Uh, I was just wondering, maybe you'd like to get a drink or something sometime."

"That would be nice," she said. "I'd like that."

"Great," I said. (Was this the dialogue of an Academy Award–winning film or what? I was ready for my close-up.)

"I can get a babysitter for tonight," she added.

I nearly leapt to my feet and screamed to the blue sky—and anyone else within earshot. I couldn't believe it was really going to happen. I'd been willing to go to any length to have this woman to myself and there she was, offering to go out with me right away. In any event, I'd managed to at least close the first deal and was well on my way to becoming the proverbial salesman of the year.

It was all Mexican, all night that first date. We went to a great Mexican restaurant for dinner and followed it up with margaritas at another fantastic Mexican restaurant just down the street. Of course I took her to the one where I knew the owner and the bartenders all treated me like a local celebrity. I wanted her to know that she wasn't out with just any jarhead, but a real important jarhead. I think I was drinking mostly to calm my nerves. That first date ended on the front steps of her house, but it was the kiss—the kiss of rebirth for me—at the end of the night that provided all the promise of things to come. It was intense; it was urgent; it was magic.

Those were good days, easy days. I had a cushy job at I Marine Expeditionary Force as one of the night senior watch officers

(SWO), which meant I only worked three to four nights a week from 2000 hours to 0800 hours (that's 8:00 PM to 8:00 AM for the uninitiated). The rest of the time was mine to pursue any number of my favorite activities, including getting to know Pam better. I'd often get off work at eight, change into bicycling clothes, and join a large group of cyclists for an intense training ride through Camp Pendleton north toward the town of San Clemente and back. Or I'd head home, take a catnap, grab my board, and head to the ocean for some surfing while the rest of San Diego worked.

September is the best time of the year in San Diego. The sun shines daily, making it ideal for any outdoor activity; the water temperature is still in the upper sixties so you don't yet need a wet suit when you surf; and the Zonies—the yearly influx of Hummer-driving, beach-crowding hordes escaping the heat of the Arizona summer who act like they own the town—have departed. I took full advantage of this as Lava and I settled into a routine of sorts.

Pam loved to surf and water-ski, too, as I found out. We shared the details of our lives: books we liked to read, the various things our dogs did to impress us, how we earned a living, and so on. I don't think Pam had ever met a Marine before, and I'm pretty sure she was the first anthropologist completing a doctoral program I'd ever run across. I was thankful she wasn't a paleontologist—she'd have used me as a subject for her dissertation.

The month of October we spent surfing every opportunity we had, then dining on one or the other surfer's culinary favorites—fish tacos or egg, potato, bacon, and cheese burritos. Ultimately, what got me additional dates with Pam and thus allowed me to continue wooing her was the occasion when, coming out of the water after a surf session, she straggled slightly behind me to "check me out" and see if I—or my back half—met with her approval (hey, her words, not mine).

Having Pam in my life altered my relationship with Lava, but it also showed me how much he'd given me and everyone over there in the anus of the world—aka Iraq. Just being able to pet him reminded us all that we were still human, still capable of feeling. Studies have shown that people with pets have lower levels of stress and anxiety. A biologist recently commented in *Newsweek* that any condition with a stress-related component can be helped by a pet: "It's providing a focus of attention that's outside of someone's self. They're actually letting you focus on them rather than focusing inward on yourself all the time."[9] Yes, science proves that it's true—pet your dog and you'll be happier and healthier.

I think the Department of Defense has finally started to accept this fact. For the first time in the history of the U.S. Army, skilled therapy dogs—provided by America's VetDogs, a subsidiary of the Guide Dog Foundation for the Blind—will be deployed to Iraq to help relieve combat stress of soldiers in the field. Two specially trained dogs will join a multidisciplinary team of army professionals to address mental health issues as they arise. The dogs, Budge and Boe, will work with members of the Eighty-fifth Medical Detachment as they work with soldiers, whether in a one-to-one or a group setting, to cope with home-front issues, sleep problems, or day-to-day operational stress. I like to think that my violation of the rules regarding pets and mascots in the combat theater, or the stories of the hundreds of other mascots, helped the DoD finally acknowledge that dogs are good for morale, not detrimental.

Maybe having Lava now—and having had him around some of the time in Iraq—is why I'm more okay than most, and when Pam walked into my life I was ready to embrace her. I no longer depend on Lava the same way, but he is still as loyal as can be. He reminds me of who I am, and where I've been, every day. I'm lucky to have him, and I hope one day it will be easier for Marines to bring back their best friends.

I heard one hopeful story recently: Lex, an approved military working dog in Iraq whose handler and best friend, Marine Corporal Dustin Lee, was killed by a mortar attack in Fallujah, was allowed early retirement to live with Lee's family. The dog wouldn't leave Lee's side when both were wounded; other Marines had to pull him away to let the medics reach Dustin. It was too late for Lee but, despite being injured by shrapnel, Lex survived. The family lobbied the Marine Corps for months afterward to bring Lex home from Iraq. I even signed an online petition urging officials at the Department of Defense to do the right thing . . . which they did. Lex returned to live with Lee's family in December 2007. I would guess he reminds the family of Dustin. His father admitted as much: "There's always going to be that missing link with Dusty gone," he said. "But part of Dusty is here with Lex."[10]

I get it. While I was still in Iraq, Lava felt like my next of kin there. So it only seemed right that he'd play as large a role in finding Pam as he did. Lava has been family since the first day I laid eyes on him. For a while there, when I first returned to the States, he was really and truly my only family.

He loves me despite my shortcomings. So does my family—my wife and children—and believe me, the shortcomings are plentiful and sometimes difficult for all. For one thing, I don't have a lot of patience and will not suffer fools.

I get agitated a little more easily than I used to, and I seem to be less tolerant of people who don't put the same importance on things as I do or who seem to take what they have for granted. On occasion I've been known to give someone a piece of my mind, too. The other day, someone parked in my reserved spot—again. There's a school adjacent to the lot where I park for work every day. Since I have the spot closest to the school, people feel it's okay—their right, even—to park in my spot while they pick their children up from school.

And it's not like they just apologize and move their cars when I tell them about it. No, they would rather argue about it.

"Oh, it's just for a minute while I'm picking up my son." Or, "I wouldn't normally do this, but there's nowhere else to park." No shit, lady, that's why I pay my landlord every month to have this spot.

Hey, excuses are like assholes—I already have one and don't need another. And if you wouldn't normally do this, then don't do it now.

I left a note for the latest violator: "To the owner of this vehicle: While I'm certain your time and feelings of self-importance are, in your mind, of greater significance than others', please understand that I have neither the interest nor the time for your discourteous behavior. Be advised that you are parked in a reserved parking spot for which I pay; by parking here you waste my time and interfere with my ability to do my job. In the future, make every effort not to confuse your sense of entitlement with others' opinions of your rude behavior. You *will* be towed at your expense." Nice, no? I did try to have the car towed, but the proper signs weren't posted, so I'll have to wait until next time.

As you can see from that lovely story, I can be somewhat irritable and have been known to lose my patience over the smallest of perceived infractions. This has gotten worse since Iraq. I can also get distracted or distant from my family, for no readily explicable reason. It fills me with shame when I realize it's happening, a feeling multiplied in spades because I have the most patient, loving, and understanding wife in the world, and there's never anything she's done—intentionally or otherwise—to warrant anything but the same in return. Maybe she knows better than I do what's going on, so she tolerates me at these times. And for that I love her even more. When we began dating, to her credit Pam didn't ask questions about what I'd seen and done in Iraq, and I didn't volunteer the information. It's as if she knew this was an area that, while not off limits, required more time to gain entrance.

Healing takes time. It's clear that Lava is not going to get past this overnight, and maybe never will. I know he's doing his best and is coping in the only way he knows how. He acts out, yes, but he doesn't possess the coping skills we do as humans.

And if *I* have whatever label you want to give me—PTSD, shell shock, soldier's heart, wacky vet syndrome—I hope that the holes blown through my soul by the sum of my experiences in Iraq can be filled by love, mine and that of my family.

CHAPTER FIVE

FEAR MAKES YOU STRONGER

"The staring eyes, the slack lips, the sleepwalker's stance . . . Mercifully, you're out of it for a while; *un*mercifully, down in the center of that numbness, though, you know you will have to come back eventually . . . The Marine in the portrait would be quick as a cat if a mortar round came shu-shu-ing in, or a fight developed. His trained instincts by now are something he can depend on, and have been developed over a long period of combat fighting. The only thing not dependable is whether, if he has bad luck, they will still save him."

—JAMES JONES, Commenting on Two-Thousand Yard Stare

Lava is the reason I'm able to admit that the same pervading fear that dogged us day in and day out in Iraq sometimes rears its ugly head here at home. The triggers for the fear might be different, to be sure, but they are just as strong. I fear that I won't live up to my children's expectations as a father; fear that I won't always be the man my beautiful wife married in the hope of sharing a full life together; fear that in the blink of an eye—much like the flash from a sniper's rifle muzzle—everything I have, Lava included, could be gone. Poof! Just like that.

I wake up some mornings covered in sweat, not sure where I am for a minute or two. I have also noticed that if I'm watching a particular type of television show—a documentary about the war, for example—I'll react to what I'm seeing, especially if there are images or reenactments of the types of things I saw or experienced while in Iraq. You have to be affected on some level if you've held the hand of a young man who nearly died in a bomb blast, no matter how tough you think you are.

Maybe the most unsettling sound in Iraq was incoming mortar and rocket fire. There was nothing you could do about that, no enemy to shoot back at. It unnerved you, made you feel helpless. There was a lot of feeling helpless in Iraq.

I never used to flinch or jump at especially suspenseful scenes in movies, but now I do. Recently I even caught myself flinching during a soldier's funeral when the honor guard fired their volley of M16s before the playing of Taps. I knew it was coming, yet something beyond my control drove me. I had never in my life experienced this inability to control my reactions to the sound of gunfire. Not on a rifle or pistol range and not in combat. So why now? I'm sure it's in some way connected to my experiences. An anticipation of what comes after the shots, and a reminder that they could hit at any moment. Let's face it: I saw a lot of body parts, and the sound of gunshots takes me back there without me even realizing it.

Have I suddenly become a coward? No, that's not it. Because while I don't act foolishly or with reckless abandon, I don't shy away from surfing big waves or skiing as many double-black-diamond runs as I can find. I've even become more aggressive in my bicycle racing, waterskiing, and wakeboarding. Those thrills are pure pleasure, because I'm not constantly looking over my shoulder for the bullet that will finally get me.

I think of how my friend Matt Hammond's life changed in an instant. He was working with Iraqi soldiers in Fallujah one night when they were approached by men who weren't immediately recognizable as insurgents. That's when it happened. One of them opened fire, killing an Iraqi soldier. The Marines fired back. A grenade got thrown, and Matt was severely wounded. The grenade managed to do so much damage to his legs that he nearly bled out right on the spot. To top it off, when the Humvee he was riding in hit a bump, the door flew open and Matt's inert, prone body was launched into the street in the middle of the night. He had to crawl his way back toward the vehicle, all the while shouting for help, before the other Marines realized what had happened and found him in the road.

And Matt's one of the lucky ones: He lived to rehab in Fallujah with Lava at his side. I know Lava helped him remember who he was before he was a warrior. Having Lava to encourage him to get out, to get some air, to feel needed, played a big role in Matt's recovery.

What is *fear* anyway? According to Merriam-Webster, it's "An unpleasant often strong emotion caused by anticipation or awareness of danger." That's pretty vague, really. Doesn't everyone react differently to danger? We all fear something, whether we admit it or not. The only true way to conquer your fears is to confront them. Look fear right in the eye and remind yourself that you're stronger. This sometimes also involves admitting that you cannot control everything. For a Marine, that's difficult. Being a Marine is all about a sense of duty, of obligation, of success. Failure is *not* an option.

A few years ago, the *Military Review* ran an article about fear and how it can affect a unit's effectiveness. I found it really fascinating, though not particularly surprising. It's a question that's been haunting military leads for as long as there have been wars. The author points out that participants in battle must react to identifiable threats as well as a pervasive, insidious uneasiness—differences that Sigmund Freud characterized as "objective anxiety" and "neurotic anxiety."

I agree with the idea that pervasive uneasiness does nothing good for a man's psyche, and that combat training should help soldiers to deal with fear, but I'm not sure there's any real way to represent this without actually experiencing it. The Army tries its best, with virtual reality preparation (which, ironically, is also being used to help traumatized veterans to overcome post-traumatic stress disorder). Still, I don't think anyone can know how his body and mind will react.

★ ★ ★

When I see Lava stretching his legs in the morning, slinking off Sean's bed (that's my stepson—you know, the kid Lava allegedly bit when Pam maneuvered to meet me?), yawning wide and blinking his kohl-lined eyes, I see myself. When Lava's face is bathed in sunlight, his eyes turn a golden brown with a distinctive depth and glint. He acts as a mirror to my soul, and I can only hope that I'm as loyal and protective of my family as he is of me. He doesn't hide his feelings; there's no pretending that he likes someone he doesn't, or vice versa.

Back in Iraq, we all stroked Lava's filthy fur in an attempt to forget the desolate, dusty terrain outside and the rough bedrolls that covered our dirt-encrusted limbs at night (or whenever we slept). I see Sean's hand linger on Lava's head sometimes, and I know his fur is soft as my new baby's skin. Lava shakes his head, ears flapping against his skull, and he opens his mouth in a doggy grin. He's a strong animal, fierce and kind. He's obviously a product of a feral coupling deep in the desert. As I've said, Lava mostly resembles a German shepherd, but he's sleeker and blonder. (It's funny that many of the dogs found on foreign soil tend to fall into this category. I like to think that Lava is more handsome than most, but I may be biased.) He's grown dramatically since he first befriended me in Fallujah, when he was a tiny ball of fur that fit into my hand—or my boot. He went through an odd big-eared phase in the time we were apart. I was struck by how much bigger his head was than his body when he first arrived in the States, with a tail that moved his entire being. That hadn't changed one bit.

Lava's jaunty belief in life itself helped me accept that my fears, from mortal to romantic, were part of the fabric of my life. The anxieties of every single moment of my time in Iraq were alleviated by thoughts of Lava's crazy antics. My insecurities about Pam were equally buoyed by the fact that Lava thought I was the greatest thing since sliced bread. Sure, he's a dog, but he's got good taste. I fell hard for Pam, and I was able to be a man she could imagine spending her life with because Lava showed me what it means to be open to life.

On the battlefield that is Iraq, we do not always find who we're looking for, but we are always accompanied by the fear that they will find us first. A thousand-yard stare is burned into us after months of dancing this waltz with the fear and uncertainty that each day and night bring. The enemy looks exactly like the innocent noncombatant smoking a cigarette at the Internet café down the street. One military-aged adult male is indistinguishable from the next—and it's not always a male who is waiting with a death machine strapped on. Women, children, dogs, you name it, can be suicide bombers. Because you can never be sure of who is the good native and who is the bad, it's nearly impossible to confront your fear head-on until that terrifying moment when the proverbial shit has, indeed, hit the fan. To tell the truth, it's almost a relief when that happens and you can channel all that aggression into your fight.

Let's face it, to a bunch of Marines and soldiers just off the plane in Iraq from Oklahoma or Indiana or even California, one bearded guy looks just like the next, all wearing the exact same clothing—until one of them pulls an AK-47. This assault rifle, the preferred weapon of our enemy, was developed during World War II and is compact, easy to use, and incredibly reliable. It is at once a beautiful and an ugly thing to behold because it is designed for one thing only: killing. And it sure looks the part, with its wood or steel buttstock and hand guard, its black steel barrel and wood grips, and its ability to cycle round after round of automatic fire without jamming, even with the introduction of foreign matter to the weapon. This is the weapon that appears from beneath the folds of a garment and suddenly releases a hailstorm of bullets and RPGs. Now you've got to react and rely on your training and instincts with no time to think. You confront that fear with your own automatic weapon and your automatic response.

In situations like these, Marines are trained to act/react and *not* to think. Thinking will get you killed. If you think too hard about what you should do with someone in your face, if you worry too much about what side he's on, you die. It's just like on the rifle range—the target pops up and you shoot without thinking, but you do so in Iraq because you *know* it's a bad guy and if you don't react fast enough or with enough deadly force, they'll be holding a memorial service for you back at Camp Pendleton or Camp Lejeune, handing a folded flag and posthumous Purple Heart to Mom and Dad. Not only that, but the Corps invests a lot of time and money in our training and equipment, ensuring that we're the finest fighting force in the world. How do you think it looks when we're taken out by some jackass wearing a "man dress" because we took the time to think rather than rely on our instincts and training? Not good, my friends, not good.

And don't tell me, by the way, that I'm being racist. No one wants to befriend someone you might have to kill in the next minute, or who might open fire on you and your best friend.

Initially, there's the fear of the firefight itself as it begins, but also a sense of relief that at least you're doing something. This fear is subsequently replaced by the fear of letting down your men, which lasts until the shooting is over and you've had a chance to allow the adrenaline to recede to that place it goes and the shaking starts, when you realize you've come within inches of dying (yet again). There's the fear of the unknown, as in being on patrol and not knowing when the sniper's bullet will find its mark or the IED will anonymously scatter your body fragments to the four points of the compass. These are real fears. This is not the branch brushing the window in a storm. This is not a harmless ant crawling across your hand during a picnic in the park with your best gal on a sunny afternoon.

So how does the Marine or soldier overcome such fears? What makes the warrior, a person of the same flesh and blood and bones as the rest of the human race, continue on? How can he bring himself to walk that patrol, breach the door behind which the enemy lies in wait, or rise up and expose himself during a firefight? It is the sense of duty, obligation, and responsibility for his fellow Marine or soldier that allows—no, requires and compels—him to do so. When you're confronted with fear in combat, you face that fear and fight back, much as you do when confronted with the enemy. You allow your fear in, but push it to the back of your subconscious, stomping on it as you would a cockroach or your enemy.

When it's all said and done—the bullets and RPGs have subsided, you've taken a head count, and you have a moment to reflect on those dead and wounded, as well as the events of which you just seconds earlier were a part—that's when the realization sets in that but for the grace of God, that poor sonofabitch in the body bag could be you. The fear is that you've got to do it all over again, and each time out could be your last. How many times can you be only inches from death? What are the odds that you'll come away unscathed next time? I think the percentages must diminish exponentially with each firefight, each patrol. The level of fear doesn't change, but how you respond to it emotionally—after the adrenaline has drained away—does.

Lava continues to achieve the same level of ferociousness every time someone rings the doorbell, but after surviving time and again he must feel a sense of pride—a sense of accomplishment— as the person backs away from the door. He keeps on going. I like that he's so consistent, like a cuddly mascot version of a US Marine. He keeps moving. Honor, obligation, and duty keep him, keep all of us, moving.

CHAPTER SIX

WHAT YOU ARE IN THE DARK

"Some people spend an entire lifetime wondering if they made a difference in the world. The Marines don't have that problem."

—RONALD REAGAN

O nce you make it through the soul-crushing, backbreaking days of training to be a Marine, you are handed your mind back should you wish to use it. You are taught to do everything a certain way, to think in terms of your team at all times, to become the honor, courage, and commitment you've learned, but with a sense of individuality, that sometimes means you admit fear or break rules. Ironically, most people think that Marines don't think for themselves; the Marine Corps actually reminds all of us of that in the code we know by heart. In reality, the Corps doesn't want automata, robots without higher intelligence who would just play Follow-the-Leader like lambs to the slaughter or lemmings to the sea. If that's your idea of leadership, join the army. No, Mother Corps believes not only that every Marine is a rifleman, but that every Marine is capable of being an effective leader. And to lead effectively, especially when the shit has truly hit the fan, you must be able to improvise, adapt, and overcome. Let's see R2-D2 do that shit.

There is room for fear in bravery. But if you rely on your training, then you have the tools to accept and overcome that fear in the face of the worst and most improbable odds. Consider this government description of Marines:

> Why are U.S. Marines considered the world's premier warriors? Why? What puts the Marine Corps above the rest? Other military services have rigorous training and weapons of equal or greater lethality. So, why do U.S. Marines stand head and shoulders above the crowd?
>
> The truth lies in the individual Marine. He (or she) did not *join* the Marines. Roughly 40,000 try each year. Those who survive the crucible of Marine basic training have been sculpted in mind and body. They have *become* Marines.
>
> Once he has *earned the title* and entered the Brotherhood of Marines, a new warrior must draw upon the legacy of his Corps. Therein lies his strength. In return, the strength of the Corps lies in the individual Marine. The *character* (often defined as "what you are in the dark") of these warriors is defined by the three constant Corps Values: honor, courage, and commitment.
>
> **Honor**: Honor requires each Marine to exemplify the ultimate standard in ethical and moral conduct. Honor is many things; honor requires many things. A U.S. Marine must never lie, never cheat, never steal,

but that is not enough. Much more is required. Each Marine must cling to an uncompromising code of *personal integrity,* accountable for his actions and holding others accountable for theirs. And, above all, honor mandates that a Marine never sully the reputation of his Corps.

Courage: Simply stated, courage is honor in action—and more. Courage is moral strength, the will to heed the inner voice of conscience, the will to do what is right regardless of the conduct of others. It is mental discipline, an adherence to a higher standard. Courage means willingness to take a stand for what is right in spite of adverse consequences. This courage, throughout the history of the Corps, has sustained Marines during the chaos, perils, and hardships of combat. And each day, it enables each Marine to look in the mirror—and smile.

Commitment: Total dedication to Corps and Country. Gung-ho Marine teamwork. All for one, one for all. By whatever name or cliché, commitment is a combination of (1) selfless determination and (2) a relentless dedication to excellence. Marines never give up, never give in, never willingly accept second best. Excellence is always the goal. And, when their active duty days are over, Marines remain reserve Marines, retired Marines, or Marine veterans. There is no such thing as an ex-Marine or former Marine. Once a Marine, always a Marine. Commitment never dies.

The three Corps Values: honor, courage, commitment. They make up the bedrock of the character of each individual Marine. They are the foundation of his Corps. These three values, handed down from generation to generation, have made U.S.

Marines the Warrior Elite. The U.S. Marine Corps: the most respected and revered fighting force on earth.[12]

Lava doesn't have that training. But you better believe he's got *character*. He was brave as hell and continued to impress me with his will to survive. I knew he was terrified from the moment he laid eyes on the U.S. Marines right up until the moment he got on that plane headed for America. He knew fear the night I first encountered him at the Lava Dog command post in Fallujah when, without thinking, I kicked and sent him flying across the floor after he chewed on my bootlaces. I could see it in his eyes as clear as day. Yet he mustered as much courage as five pounds of flea-bitten mongrel possibly can and charged right back at me, full of himself and his puppy's toughness.

That's what we're taught after all, isn't it? To muster up our courage in the face of adversity. To not let fear get the best of us. Combatants live in constant fear, yet we don't—won't/can't/for fear of ridicule/all of the above—admit it. The irony is stunning. Instead, we put on displays of courage, which is merely the ability to confront and overcome our fears. Yes, there are truly brave people in the world, but I don't count myself among them. I have convictions, and the courage of my convictions allows me to overcome my fears and act in a courageous manner without making a complete fool of myself in combat. Why, it's not manly to be afraid. *Big boys don't cry,* we're told. I'm here to tell you that's *bullshit*!

I'm worried about my fellow veterans. I'm concerned that most of the men I fought alongside are afraid to reveal their weaknesses. Even the Department of Defense Task Force on mental health is concerned, declaring in 2007,

"The costs of military service are substantial. Many costs are readily apparent; others are less apparent but no less important. Among the most pervasive and potentially disabling consequences of these costs is the threat to the psychological health of our nation's fighting forces, their families, and their survivors."

A war like Iraq is bound to have repercussions. Is it a lack of courage to admit you don't like wiping another man's brains from your boots? Is your commitment failing when you decline to attend a talk about mental health and choose instead to hit the local tavern with the hot girl you dated in high school? We're taught to care as much about our pack—actually more about the well-being of the group—than of ourselves. The Warrior Elite are fighting individual wars these days; from desolate, backwater towns across the Midwest to anonymous cities across the country, men and women are alone and unwilling to talk about it. I can understand that.

I admit I had plenty of fear, and it wasn't just my fear of failing the Marines to whom I'd promised Lava would have a home in the United States. It became a more specific fear of failing Lava. After all, I'd:

1. Removed him from the city of Fallujah. (What if I'd left him there to suffer the same fate as so many other stray and feral dogs and cats?)

2. Brought him to Camp Fallujah, the Marine base located seven kilometers outside the city. (What would happen if there was no one to care for him?)

3. Left him in the hands of the commanding general's personal security detail, entrusting them with his life. (Would the DoD contractors charged with ridding the bases of unwanted and nonmilitary animals get him before the Marines could spirit him away?)

4. Arranged his transfer from Camp Fallujah to Baghdad, where he would live with Anne Garrels at the NPR compound. (What if the Marines encountered the enemy during their trip to Baghdad and had to abandon Lava?)

5. Attempted "exfiltration" via the Jordanian border in the back of a courier's Suburban. (What if the driver, who was so terrified of Lava, decided it would be easier just to abandon him at the side of the road and collect his money, claiming the Jordanians had confiscated and killed the mongrel?)

6. Left Iraq at the end of my tour without Lava, who remained in Baghdad, his fate uncertain. (Would he ever end up in the United States? Would the people caring for him get tired of helping him?)

Why did I have so much fear and angst over the fate of one stupid dog? I mean, he was just a dog, and I was in clear violation of the rules even giving this mutt one MRE, much less trying to arrange his safe passage to America. Was it that I actually thought I had a chance of saving him? That while I clearly wasn't going to save every man, woman, and child in that godforsaken land, I was damn well going to keep my promise to my men and to this dog because *I thought I actually could*?

Yeah, that sounds about right. Not only that, but I figured at that point in the war, Lava was far more likely to take advantage of being saved than any of the Iraqis I'd met. That first time Lava crawled into my bag with me, and I held him as he looked at me with those raccoon eyes and licked my face—then and there he had me. If *I* didn't know then that I'd be doing all I could to save him, I think Lava somehow did.

Lava won my heart and mind. He was now an important part of my life, not just for what he symbolized—the heart and soul, the humanity of all of us on this earth, Iraqi, American, everyone—but for what he'd come to mean to me and for the pure joy and escape he provided me during those fleeting moments we had together. The Iraqis had not fallen in love with us; they didn't even seem to want us there most of the time. Lava was different. He was always as happy to see me as I was to see him.

I think I talk about my emotions now because Lava has shown me that part of my *personal integrity* is to be true to those feelings. They exist. Fear exists. Anger is there. Sadness. Yes. His friendship and the love of my family help alleviate the intensity, but it's all there under the surface. I'm working to make sure there's some release from time to time. Part of that is simply allowing myself to have my feelings. The Marine Corps may have turned me into an efficient killing machine, but it didn't take my heart.

Or my dog.

I never experienced a panic attack or passed out in fear. No, I never crapped myself, despite the quiet glee with which people ask me that question. In his classic Vietnam book, *Dispatches*, Michael Herr nails the scene of the curious outsider asking his curiosity-killed-the-cat questions to a bunch of grunts:

"What does it look like when a man gets hit in the balls?" the new man said, as though it were the question he'd really meant to ask all along and it came as close as you could get to a breach of taste in that room, palpable embarrassment all around . . .

No, there weren't physical symptoms for me, but you bet my mind raced before combat. The imminent danger of an IED, enemy mortar, or sniper ending my life in some horribly painful manner, my limbs being torn from my body, or my head evaporating in an explosive spray of the proverbial pink mist, haunted me. I'd never get to see the ocean again, or to surf, or to have a cigar with my best friend, Eric. Fear of coming back with missing limbs—who would love me like that? Fury that it might happen to me. Sadness at the thought of the pain my parents would suffer if I didn't make it back. My jaw tenses just thinking of what might have happened to Lava after I left him with the CG's PSD Marines the night I flew to Balad, and then again the night I left for the Syrian border.

I didn't have control over whether Lava lived or died. I couldn't physically protect him or save him. I couldn't handle that. You see, I have what psychologists call a Type A personality (my wife calls it a Type A personality *disorder*) and am thus prone to being impatient, excessively time-conscious, insecure about my status, highly competitive, hostile, aggressive, and incapable of relaxation. But enough about me. What, there's more? Type A individuals are often highly achieving workaholics (but we don't go to 12-step meetings) who multitask, drive themselves with deadlines, and are unhappy about the smallest of delays. (*What's taking so long with that nonfat-no-whip-soy-added-shot-extra-hot grande latte in a tall cup?* Wait, that's not Type A, it's Type A-hole.) That doesn't sound too bad, does it?

But how about this last part? People with the Type A personality are not incapable of showing love, affection, or other types of nonpessimistic behavior. Ah, that's more like it. See, I am human after all. Well, at least where Lava and my family are concerned. But because of my Type A personality, I'm unable to respond adequately to the fear I feel for Lava's safety because I don't have the proper tools (isn't that the popular, politically correct jargon these days?—or should I just come out and say *I'm emotionally incapable?*).

It's not easy. I like to bottle up my fear and not let anyone see it. I am a master at keeping it to myself and presenting a cold, hard veneer that is impenetrable even to depleted-uranium, armor-piercing bullets. *Nothing can break me down and I'll be damned if I'm gonna let anyone or anything penetrate this protective shell I've built for myself. This is war, dammit, and war's hell,* et cetera, et cetera, et cetera. I really can play that game, and I'm good at it. Lava has always broken the facade, though.

Does it make me weak, somehow, after I'd kept all my worries about Lava bottled up for days, weeks, months during his long journey to America (it wasn't an easy trip for him, and there were times when he almost didn't make it to his next doggy treat [twelve hours in a car during a drive to the Jordanian border where he was refused entry; another drive down IED alley, the road from Baghdad to the Baghdad International Airport; and getting through Jordanian customs on a forged international puppy passport]) that when I got the phone call from John Van Zante of the Helen Woodward Animal Center, who flew to Chicago to meet Lava's plane in the United States, and Lava finally set his paws on American soil . . . I hung up the phone and cried like a little kid for one of the only times in my adult life? I guess you macho guys out there—the ones who've never fought for your lives, you high-school bullies—can say it does if you want. If it makes you feel better about yourselves and your own insecurities.

It wasn't for Lava alone that I was crying. I see now that it was my way to tap into the pain and anxiety I'd tried so hard to suppress. It was the release of everything I'd bottled up inside for six and a half months, not wanting to expose my soft underbelly as a sign of weakness to myself, my Marines, the Iraqis we led in Fallujah. It was the sadness I finally let myself feel for the young Marines I'd seen wounded or killed in combat before they ever had a chance at a real life, a life that I have today, filled with happiness and wonderment at the miracle of life that is embodied by my one-year-old son.

★ ★ ★

My fears now aren't about things that will kill me or my best friend, but they're no less important. I worry—fear—that I won't set the right example as a husband and father for my sons to emulate, that my wife will stop loving me, that I won't earn enough money to care for my family, that I won't be able to afford to one day send my son to the college of his choice, that my books won't sell. These are legitimate and real concerns, but they're not likely fatal.

I work to be the best husband and father I possibly can be to my wife and children. I strive to set the example for my boys of what a man can and should be. You stand up for what you believe in, have confidence in yourself, and treat others fairly—and, when necessary, with firmness. I teach them to act with honor and dignity, and to defend those who are weaker. I teach them these things so that when they find themselves in a fearful situation—whether it's a spider crawling across their hand in the dark or combat in some foreign land—they'll have the tools to cope with and confront their fears. I hope I pass down the lessons I've learned about honor, courage, and commitment. That each person has to find his own definition of those things, and stand by it. That doing the right thing is more important than blindly following rules.

Finally, I try my best to teach them that it's okay to say you're afraid.

Dear Lt. Col. Kopelman:

Recently I finished reading From Baghdad, With Love. It is a remarkable account of a lot of people on both sides of the fence, so to speak, who put aside personal safety, comfort, rules, and financial considerations to make sure this rascally puppy, Lava, would eventually be able to have a carefree life in the United States.

Many times in the book you seemed to be making apologies for a weakness as a softhearted, compassionate human being because you were supposed to be the epitome of the hardhearted, hard-boiled, no-nonsense U.S. Marine officer. My assessment is that sort of conduct did not show weakness but actually a strength seldom seen in today's world.

I was particularly drawn to the Lava story because I am an 84-year-old WWII veteran and because I, too, rescued a German shepherd puppy and brought her home at the end of the war. She (I named her

Dusty and Robbie

Dusty) was 6 to 8 weeks old when I found her running loose on the streets in Germany, hungry and scared, and with some difficulty (but certainly nothing compared with yours attendant to Lava) keeping and caring for her, I managed to get her to my home in Michigan.

Dusty was delivered to my parents at my home in Lansing, Michigan, about a week and a half before I got home after being discharged; we had been separated for approximately two months. Therefore, I can relate to your experience when you were reunited with Lava in San Diego. I had arrived in Lansing by train about 2:00 AM and got to my home at 3:00 AM. Dusty was in our backyard in her shipping crate which my parents had used for a kennel. When she heard my usual whistle call, she raised such a ruckus that the neighbors all around knew I must be home. At that time, being much younger than you, I had no trouble showing my emotions at the reunion and I damn well didn't care who was aware of the tears and my love for Dusty.

I send my thanks and love to all those who helped to rescue Lava: the tough, softhearted Lava Dogs, Sam and other Iraqis who "crossed lines" to enter into the overall effort, Anne and all those across the U.S. who sidetracked daily routines to make Lava their priority.

Most sincerely,

Robert L. "Robbie" Robinson

Technician, 8th Armored Division, Ninth Army

CHAPTER SEVEN

HOW THE ROUTINE OF STAYING ALIVE CAN KEEP YOU SANE

"The following is a brief schedule of the regular routine: At 5 A.M. the *reveille* is beaten, the several companies are formed, and the roll is called by the First Sergeants. At 5½ o'clock company drills take place.These drills are very severe and continue for an hour. At 7 o'clock the Battalion is marched down to the mess-hall for breakfast when some two hundred and fifty hungry individuals quickly dispose of the 'hash' and bread . . . ."
—"AFFAIRS AT WEST POINT," *THE NEW YORK TIMES*, AUGUST 4, 1860

Fear and boredom are the warrior's biggest enemies. Lava helped keep both at bay back when I was in Iraq fighting. He needed us to be responsible and strong for him. When he was quaking in mortal fear (and even when he was masking it), I knew he was scared. Peeing on the floor was a direct tell. Taking care of him was something we could do above and beyond protecting our country and one another, risking death—or worse, death without purpose—in the process. It meant feeding him and watching that he didn't crawl under the gate and become lost among the other soulless animals doing whatever was necessary to survive in the wasteland of Fallujah.

Now I have a wife and two sons to keep me busy but Lava still manages to keep me entertained and on track. It's the best way I know to keep the demons at a distance. That and exercise.

Dogs like routine. So do Marines.

Marines easily adapt to and become part of a routine. In recruit training and officer candidate school, we are indoctrinated into a daily routine that rarely varies. You know you're going to wake up at a given time. You'll eat at roughly the same time each day. You'll be in bed at the same time every night. So routine is imprinted in our military DNA early on and stays with us during our careers. It's not something that leads to complacency or boredom. In fact, the routine is a way to get us used to repetitive activity without complacency setting in. It tells us—with or without an alarm clock—when it's time to get our asses out of the rack and get on with the day.

You don't have to sweat the same details most civilians do when you are in the military. But you do pay attention to detail because failure to do so could lead to severe bodily injury or death to you or, worse, your squad mates.

You work the hours you're told to work (meaning you work until the work is done even if that's twenty-four hours straight or more), you do the tasks you're assigned, you live where you're told to live, and you deploy where and when you're told to deploy. And you don't have to worry about what you're going to wear to work in the morning—they've got that figured out, too. It may be hard for a civilian to understand, but this sort of tight routine actually frees you to focus on the bigger picture—the needs of your Marines, the Corps as a whole, and the country. And I want to die knowing that I did my part, to leave my family proud of me for that. Self-discipline, sacrifice, loyalty, and obedience are the bulwarks of a Marine's life. You start learning that in boot camp, and if you make it through—many recruits and officer candidates do not—you will learn the value of rigid routine and absolute control. Marine boot camp is the most challenging basic training in any of the branches of the armed forces.

When a kid decides to become a Marine, he goes to a recruiter, who will typically tell him that he really doesn't have what it takes. He'll only make the kid a poolee (someone waiting to go to boot camp) after the kid has proven his undying dedication to the Corps. There are no signing bonuses, à la the army and the navy. The signing bonus is you get to be a Marine, should you endure the rigors of boot camp, the physical and intellectual (if you can use that word here) requirements of which are higher for Marine recruits than for those in the other services. Consider the physical fitness test: In the army they run two miles; the Marines run three. 'Nuff said. (Never mind the navy, who run only a mile and a half and who have the option of a swim; or the Air Force, where if you're not medically cleared to run, you can ride a stationary bike.) The training programs in each branch of the military are scientifically and psychologically designed to tear apart the civilian and build from the ground up a proud, physically fit, and dedicated member of the United States Armed Forces. You get so used to being disciplined, in fact, that it can be extremely difficult to come back to the less structured, everyday life that most civilians lead.

Right from the first days at boot camp, you discover that there's a plan for everything, that everything is done by the numbers—from the simple process of washing eating utensils to putting on your "pro-mask," or field protective gas mask.

Here are directions for "Cleaning Individual Mess Gear":

1. **EQUIPMENT REQUIRED.** Four corrugated cans or other similar containers placed in a row are required for washing mess gear. The first can contains hot soapy water and is used as a prewash; the second can contains hot soapy water (150 degrees F) for a second wash; and the third and fourth cans contain clear water which is kept boiling (rolling boil) throughout the work period. Long-handled wash brushes and a garbage can or pit are also needed. Additional cans may be used for garbage and waste.

2. **PROCEDURES FOR CLEANING MESS GEAR**
A: Scrape the food particles from eating utensils into a garbage can.
B: Using the long handled brush provided, wash the eating utensils in the first container of hot soapy water.
C: Using the long handled brush provided, wash the eating utensils in the second container of hot soapy water.

D: Immerse the eating utensils in the first container of clear boiling water for approximately 30 seconds.

E: Immerse the eating utensils in the second container of clear boiling water for approximately 30 seconds.

F: Shake the eating utensils to remove the excess water. Check to ensure that the eating utensils are clean. If not, repeat the washing cycle.

G: Allow to air dry.

Then there's my all-time favorite procedure: donning the gas mask, the full description of which follows. By the time you finish going through all the steps, you'll have passed out from lack of oxygen, having held your breath for two minutes while your heart rate accelerates, the sense of urgency heightens, and thoughts of horribly disfiguring sores arising on your body fill your thoughts as the NBC (Nuclear, Biological, Chemical) instructor yells, "Gas, gas, gas!" Or worse, as the gas is actually falling from a Scud missile in the middle of the desert.

I finally realized the hilarity of all this during just such a drill in Kuwait before the Iraq invasion in March 2003. I witnessed the Marine Expeditionary Unit command-element Marines—many of whom were Marines in uniform and training only; the only input most had to the war effort was coming up with a tactical name for our unit—acting like a bunch of monkeys fucking a football as they fell over themselves and one another in an effort to don the pro-mask while making a terror-filled dash for the Scud bunkers. It was all-out bedlam as each Marine tried to be the first to exit our tents for the safety of the sandbag-encased concrete bunkers, each convinced that without the mask he'd die in this godforsaken shithole, choking and gagging on one lethal poison gas or another, convulsing on the ground in a version of what we liked to call the funky chicken.

This was one of the few times I got to witness leadership from the front with the command's most senior officers leading the charge, stiff-arming the enlisted men out of their way, looking more like Heisman Trophy statues than Marine officers.

Ultimately the command settled on the moniker Task Force Yankee, because the commanding officer was from New York and was a Yankees fan. Imagine the jokes. Or you could just read them on the outhouse walls: TASK FORCE YANKEE GO HOME! TF YANKEE MY WANKEE!

But I digress.

DONNING AND CLEARING THE FIELD PROTECTIVE MASK. Upon hearing or seeing the alarm for gas:

a. Stop breathing. *(Yeah, right. Now that you're about to die a gruesome death and your adrenaline is pumping, you're gonna stop breathing.)*

b. Remove your headgear with your right hand and open your carrier with your left hand. Place headgear as directed. *(Don't even think about doing this the other way around.)*

c. Hold the carrier open with your left hand; grasp the facepiece just below the eyepieces and remove the mask with your right hand. *(What really happens is you drop the headgear on the ground, er, deck.)*

d. Grasp the facepiece with both hands, sliding your thumbs up inside the facepiece under the lower head harness straps. Lift your chin slightly. *(Just put the fucker on, dammit!)*

e. Seat the chin pocket of the facepiece firmly on the chin. Bring head harness smoothly over head, ensuring that the head harness straps are straight and the head pad is centered.

f. Smooth the edges of the facepiece on your face with upward and backward motion of hands, pressing out all bulges to secure an airtight seal.

g. Close the outlet valve by cupping the heel of your right hand firmly over the opening; blow hard to clear agent from the facepiece.

h. Block air inlet holes of the filter elements, shutting off the air supply. When you inhale, the facepiece should collapse.

i. Resume breathing (give the alarm).

You get the picture. The belief—at least in Marine Corps boot camp and officer candidate school—is that learning the new routine is so difficult, especially when a drill instructor or sergeant instructor puts a metal trash can on your head and bangs on it while yelling at you (I've actually seen this happen and you laugh as much at your good fortune that it's not you as you do at the humor of it all), that they actually paint yellow footprints on the ground so you'll know where to stand.

Not only that, but if you're a Marine, you have to learn an entirely new language. You don't go upstairs, you go "topside." You don't go downstairs, you go "down below." Your bunk becomes a "rack." The latrine is a "head." The floor is a "deck." The walls are "bulkheads." The windows are "portholes." The ceiling is an "overhead." You face "forward." Your ass is "aft." Left is "port" and right is "starboard." You're thinking this all sounds very nautical, and it is, because the Marines are a part of the Department of the Navy—the men's department. You are on a ship to nowhere, even when your tent is on the shifting sands of the desert. Questions are not welcomed.

Is it any wonder that it's so difficult to return to a world in which everyone's opinion is respected? Where we're all "on the same page"? Where hours are spent swirling and sipping wine? No wonder the USMC is known as "The Few. The Proud. The Marines." (A slogan that, incidentally, was recently enshrined on Madison Avenue's Advertising Walk of Fame.)

What I'm trying to say is that for the disciplined Marines of the Lava Dogs and the I MEF commanding general's personal security detail, Lava was both a distraction and another cog in the machine, but one that we alone could save.

I can assure you that Lava's routine was in no way boring to anyone, and somehow I became as involved in it as anyone else in Iraq, simply because it was there to be had, and came equipped with a fuzzy ball of charm and bravado. In Iraq, I mostly facilitated Lava's care via e-mail (and phone calls when I could). I had to keep my promise to the Marines, remember, and even though I was mostly somewhere—anywhere—other than with Lava, I had to make sure that others would establish the routine for him and see to his care and feeding.

I firmly believe that the Marines and civilians who were involved with Lava on a daily basis found that the routine of feeding, exercising, and hiding the little guy offered tremendous relief from all the tedium, anxiety, boredom, and fear related to combat or living in a combat zone—and just the right amount of distraction from the routine of staying alive to help them maintain their sanity. It allowed the men and women who were involved with Lava to stay alive by not *fixating* on doing so. Does that make sense? Maybe you had to be there.

Things aren't so different now, as far as Lava and I are concerned. I still need to be kept busy, to focus on the future rather than the past. To not fixate on staying alive (although the only shots anyone takes at me now are critiques of my books) or on what I've been through (though my experiences haven't been as horrific as what many others have seen and done). And Lava? Well, let's just say that I'm trying to get him to move on. The simplest way for me to do that is to keep on going, keep him scheduled, try to avoid surprises (too bad the cable guy is so unpredictable), and make sure he's eating well, sleeping, and exercising. Because if I don't, everybody pays.

Maybe Lava's problem is that he never got to attend a post-mission debriefing and therefore never had a chance to vent and share his emotional reactions to the trauma. Yes, even our experiences of being shot at or killing or watching the guy next to us get killed were processed into a precisely packaged military-coordinated routine.

The theory, according to the army, is that these sorts of debriefings will enhance morale and unit cohesion and reduce "battle fatigue." Even if a soldier behaves like someone suffering from severe stress, the military tries to get him back on that horse, pronto. Proximity—Immediacy—Expectancy—Simplicity

(PIES) is put into place: The army addresses the issues (if you can call watching your best buddy's head being blown off by an IED an "issue") as close to the men's unit and as quickly as possible. Soldiers are told that their feelings are normal and they can expect to return to their unit shortly. The experience of battle and its aftermath is treated like a combination of a really, really bad bout of flu mixed in with having just been mugged. And if you believe what you read in the army brochures, all the soldier needs to do is get plenty of rest, eat, and talk about what happened.

We don't have time for that in the Marine Corps (we're too small and too busy) but the army makes the time for its people. I've gotta give 'em credit: one thing the army does better than the Corps is touchy-feely. (Operation Solace, a program the army developed to help Pentagon personnel and their families cope with the experience and associated trauma of the 9/11 attacks, uses PIES.)

Lava has his own form of PIES that you or I would call "sweating out the demons," accomplished through intense, hard-core exercise. Lava always seems happiest when he's romping in the park or on a run with my wife. He's focused by the exertion, and his mind doesn't wander or jump to conclusions the way it otherwise might. Certainly exercise has helped me. Whether I'm skiing, surfing, or racing my bicycle, I find that the concentration required helps me block out any distractions or negative thoughts. There is nothing remotely associated with Fallujah or Iraq in my brain when I'm on a wave or skiing a bump run, the cold crisp mountain air filling my lungs. I'm carried away to another place entirely, free at last to drop my pack and forget the demons that chase me in the night.

Paddling out at a favorite surf break with my wife erases all cares, and even if there are fifty other surfers trying to drop on the same wave . . . they might as well not exist. I'm thinking about the wave and watching the sets come in and wondering if she's going to catch it, too, when suddenly it's there and I'm on top of it, and that's what matters.

Likewise, when I'm racing my bike and my body and brain are on the brink of oxygen deprivation, it's all I can do to hang on and not crash at thirty-plus miles per hour. The rush is incredible, exhilarating, riding scant inches away from racers to my left and right, front and back. The endorphins kick in, the body tenses, the senses come alive, and I'm performing at the peak of my physical abilities. I don't have time to think about what might have been, had that rocket exploded fifty feet closer. If you think about almost dying in Iraq while you're racing a bicycle at breakneck speed in a Southern California criterium, you're sure to crash and take several of your teammates and opponents with you. It demands your complete attention and respect for the speed of the peloton, the proximity of other racers, and the density of the pavement below you.

Lava may not have the benefit of all these various physical activities, but I'm pretty sure he finds the same rush by "dominating" (read: humping) the neighborhood golden retrievers.

Routine, distraction, avoidance, call it what you want. Unfortunately, it doesn't always work as well as I would like. I can still explode at the slightest provocation, especially when I'm caught off guard. Take what happened the other night. I screwed up big-time. I was unfairly hard on my stepson when he answered a simple yes-or-no question in what I perceived to be a frustrated, impatient, and disrespectful tone of voice. It was probably nothing, and a grown man should be able to overlook these things.

I'd just finished a great indoor training session with a couple of teammates from my bicycle racing team and was feeling really good. But as I was driving up our street (we live on a one-way street) some jackass came barreling down it in the wrong direction. This happens all too frequently, and with so many small children and dogs and cats on the street, it's a serious problem. Kids aren't looking for, or expecting, cars coming the wrong way.

So I blocked his way. The asshole pulled into a driveway. I thought he'd get out of the car to go into the house, at which time I could nicely explain the dangers of coming down our street the wrong way. Instead he waited for me to park and then took off. I tried to get in his way, but he was going too fast, and when I yelled, he blared his horn. That's not a big deal, really, except it was nearly nine o'clock at night, and people don't want that kind of disturbance in an otherwise peaceful neighborhood. I was, of course, completely pissed off now that this guy thought that what he had to do and where he had to go was more important than having the slightest modicum of respect for my street and my neighbors, and the traffic laws that are in place to provide safety for my children and those of my neighbors.

If I'd been holding anything other than my phone, I'd have thrown it at his car.

I was pumped up and pissed off by the time I walked into my house. I knew my stepson had a ton of homework, and the first thing I wanted to know was if he'd been able to get it done.

"Hey, buddy, did you finish your homework?" I asked.

"Ye-eessss," was the reply.

Now, that is certainly the appropriate word in this case—well, one of the two suitable ones—but it was the tone I couldn't tolerate. I mean, when did the word "yes" become multi-syllabic? I guess I snapped. I lifted his chin with my hand—for emphasis and to make sure he'd be looking me in the eye—and in my best imitation of my father said, "Don't you ever, ever talk that way to me or any other adult again. I've had enough of your disrespectful tone, pal, and it won't be tolerated for even one second in this house. I asked you a simple question that required nothing more than a simple answer. Nothing more. You learn to stow your frustration. You can talk to your friends that way, but not to me, not to your mother, and not to your teacher. Am I clear?"

His reply—crying.

There's nothing more wrenching in the world than seeing your child unhappy. The pain multiplies exponentially when you're the one who caused it. Of course I apologized, but I couldn't shake the sense that I was truly an asshole. He's nine years old. His life should be a party, and there I was doing everything I could to piss on it. Shoot me now.

I can blame it on the Land Rover, I suppose. (Where have you heard that phrase before? Is my life a series of screwups destined to repeat again and again?) But what good would blame do? Would it assuage my guilt? Would it make my stepson feel any better? I gotta tell you, as bad as I felt that night, the next morning was even worse. Because as much of a dick as I was to him, when I woke him for school he was all smiles. It was as if nothing had happened and we were best buddies again. The knife in my heart twisted at least five times.

I have these moments, unfortunately, that I can only describe as outbursts. I don't know when they're going to come, or why, but they do. Fortunately, they're not violent—but they are angry. I don't know exactly what triggers them. I suspect it's due in large part to the lack of respect I have for so many people and the way they excuse certain mistakes they've made and their lack of understanding for the sacrifices my fellow Marines, soldiers, sailors, and airmen have made on behalf of this country. I know that's not 100 percent fair. People can't possibly know that about me, especially when I live in a place like La Jolla. They form opinions (e.g., Marines are macho thrill-seekers who can whip anyone in push-ups but haven't picked up a book in years). And in truth, some of the people I truly dislike were the only ones who said "boo" about my service to my country on Veterans' Day this past year. So what is it?

I love my stepson very much and want only the best for him. I know he's had a difficult time since his parents' divorce and I need to cut him some slack. Yet as much as I wish I could prevent my anger from surfacing and try to suppress it, there are times when I can't.

This behavior hurts my stepson; it hurts my wife; and it hurts me to the core to know that I've caused them even a moment's angst. Just as importantly, I know I'm not setting the right example. That is perhaps the most difficult part of this for me. How can I tell my boys that I expect them to behave a certain way when I model a diametrically opposite type of behavior? I worry that my baby, Mattox, will develop the wrong beliefs and ideas about what a man should be. I worry that he's seeing a grown man yell at a small boy. That he'll think it's okay to bully people who are smaller. *It's not okay, Mattox. If you're strong, you can afford to be silent. Are you listening? Do as I say, not as I do, in this instance.*

My wife tells me that I am a wonderful person, that I make everyone very happy. But I think I'm just a miserable old man who's incapable of giving back the love my family gives me. I tell her that I'm not worth wasting even an ounce of emotion on because I can't seem to stop my anger from getting the best of me. So what the hell am I to do? I don't want to lose my family, to live without my sons, to give in to the negativity that gnaws at me every day. I really try to be the best that I can be for my family, to keep them safe through the night and provide for them from the moment Lava starts his sunrise *roo-roo-roo.* I make sure that my stepson has a wholesome and healthy breakfast every morning that he's with us (believe it or not, I usually make pancakes, eggs, and orange juice) and I make his lunch every morning, too, all the way to cutting the crust off his PB&J sandwich, just the way he likes it. It's critical that I remind myself that I'm loved and capable of loving before the anger enters my body.

And then there's Lava, and the way he so often just loses it for no apparent reason. When I watch him and try to understand what's happening to him as he wrestles with the demons inside— maybe I can stop myself from losing it. Yet I worry. What if that's not enough? What if the fear I'm so comfortable admitting is actually a substitute for the rage I feel at having lost my innocence and the vehemence with which I want to save my children? What then?

Dear Mr. Kopelman,

Hello. First off I would like to introduce myself.

My name is Thomas George Martinez, I hail from Denver, Colorado, and am a specialist in the U.S. Army. In order for me to fully express my thoughts on your book I would like to share with you a story of my own.

In March of 2005 I deployed to Iraq in support of Operation Iraqi Freedom III and was assigned to a unit with the duty of being gun truck escorts. My duty stations included Talil, Scania, and Stryker but in the course of my assignment I managed to escort trucks to every major base in Iraq and have slept in a tent at each one.

Around the month of October, the stress of being in a combat situation was already starting to bear weight on my shoulders. At this time, a portion of our unit was instructed to stop gun truck missions in Talil and move to Scania for the job of gate security.

Thomas Martinez with Uno

About my third week at Scania, I noticed a group of Iraqi children (same group I saw on a regular basis) walking through a nearby field with a small motionless puppy dangling from a noose like some sort of bizarre yo-yo.

I immediately called my interpreter Alex over and had him call those kids over and ask them what the heck they were doing.

It turns out they had no use for the dog at their home so they were taking it out to the field to end its life. I told them to turn the dog over to me and go back home. Much like Lava, Uno (named after the card game that consumed our downtime) was dipped in kerosene for de-ticking, then bathed, groomed, and fed enough MREs to make a wolf pack jealous.

This small, weak, laughable excuse for a dog soon became my most loved companion and one of the best reasons I had to be in a rush to get back to my guard point.

She made me feel more at home and comfortable than most social situations I had encountered in my deployment, and I wanted nothing more than for her to be able to survive and redeploy back with me to the States. I could fill several pages with stories of my misadventures with Uno, and the memory of her still makes me smile.

Unfortunately my story doesn't end as well as yours. One day while I was off duty, Uno was seen by a general and executed on the spot. Shortly after that I rejoined the rest of my unit at Stryker to continue my original mission.

Uno represented everything I missed about being home and whenever she was around I transformed from a soldier at war to just a guy and his dog. In a

Uno as gun escort

situation as tense and life changing as war, the distraction that Uno provided for me was precious.

Your story helped remind me of similar struggles and incidents I encountered, but most importantly it reminded me of my experience with my own little yipping partner in crime.

Thank you for succeeding in saving your own little distraction. The fact that someone got to save their dog makes me feel better about my story. Even though we have seen and taken part in horrid things it can take something as simple as a puppy to make us feel most human.

I find myself with only five more days until I become a civilian again and every little piece of closure I get is precious to me. Your story was very

good and I wish you and your family all the luck in
the future.

Sincerely,
Thomas George Martinez

Specialist, U.S. Army

CHAPTER EIGHT

YOU ARE THE SUM OF YOUR EXPERIENCES

"Compared to initial screening upon returning from the Iraq war, U.S. soldiers report increased mental health concerns and needs several months after their return for problems such as *post-traumatic stress disorder* and depression, according to a study in the November 14 [2007] issue of *Journal of the American Medical Association (JAMA)*."

—JAMA

Routine and exercise help keep me sane, but I know that my experiences in Iraq have changed me. When I first got back, and Lava was enduring one private training session after another, I would just watch him and Graham Bloem, who'd helped with Lava's first day in the United States. Graham is a terrific trainer who could somehow get Lava to listen to him without ever raising his voice. He'd angle his body sideways so he looked less aggressive. He worked on what he called "resource guarding," when a dog will guard anything that he perceives as having value. It's often food, but with Lava it was also me, then Pam and Sean and Mattox. The process of coaxing Lava away from his neuroses was sort of what I imagined therapy to be like. Dog-training manuals are always big on the idea that the owner had to be trained as much as the dog, and I don't think Graham was any different. Part two of that is that I don't think I made it easy for him. He once told me, "I've worked with a lot of Marines, and it's not easy to tell a lieutenant colonel how to handle his dog, no matter what the situation."

Sometimes during the training I'd start talking about the war. Real detailed stuff. Graham would be teaching Lava to sit and stay and I'd say something about an Iraqi soldier who died. It freaked him out. He told my editor, "He'd get very intense, and sometimes I would just think, *You've seen things that no one should have to see.*" I guess if it were up to him, he'd recommend that I get myself some help. Practicing sit and stay sounds a lot easier than therapy, though. Shall we examine Lava, then?

From the outset, Lava lived a tenuous existence, having to fend for himself amid the chaos and terror of the combat around him. His need to overprotect started in Iraq. Once Lava finally made it to Baghdad to live with Anne Garrels and the folks from National Public Radio in the Red Zone (bad-guy territory), it was as though he felt some sort of obligation for their safety (especially Annie's). He took it upon himself to be not only the sounder of reveille every morning, but also everyone's vocal protector; that is, he'd be up and at 'em at the slightest provocation, and this included a thorough episode of howling every single morning during the guards' shift change—at 0500.

He never knew when, or if, he'd eat again. And when he got that opportunity, what would be his meal? I remember how he went wild when he got his first tastes of MREs. Among his favorites was the Country Captain Chicken with Buttered Noodles. It's a barely edible rehydrated "chicken patty" served with these god-awful noodles slick with a kind of wax-like coating that they try to pass off as butter. You can warm the package with a special flameless heater: Just add water and some bizarre chemical reaction makes that little pouch hot. Slip it into the bigger pouch and you've got your dinner at two hundred piping degrees. Lava didn't mind it cold—he'd faced the possibility of eating the fetid flesh of another dog or cat or the face of an insurgent recently dispatched to the great beyond by coalition forces, so spaghetti with a side of snack bread and cheese spread, topped off by blueberry-cherry cobbler, must have seemed a feast fit for a king.

He's a dog, I know, so maybe one hunk of meat is the same as another. But really, how can a human being reconcile the idea that dogs are routinely killed during war for a combination of offenses including (1) being a source of emotional support to the troops, (2) scavenging food from the bodies of dead insurgents, and (3) existing? How is that okay? When does reality become just nightmares, and when do the nightmares become your reality? There's a very fine line, I believe, and it's easily crossed with just a slight nudge. Or worse, it's completely obliterated or obscured by the fog of war, so that you come to accept the hellish life to which you've been relegated as normal.

If anyone suffers from post-traumatic stress disorder, it's got to be Lava. He can't deny it, either, like most of us humans are wont to do. I've done some reading up on this, and the fact is, most military guys will do anything to avoid going to medical. It's a fate worse than death to admit weakness. Then, on top of that, you've got to miss action. No way. Far easier to self-medicate with drugs (*prescribed or over-the-counter*) or booze. Warriors are meant to fight, not to talk or hide in bed. "WTF" is the common response to hearing that someone's gone to the doctor. In fact, pilots call the logbook they have to sign when they go to a doctor the "snivel log." Now, what red-blooded American fighting man is going to voluntarily sign that thing?

Lava, on the other hand, is nothing but an empty vessel waiting for my analysis. And I've decided. He's got it, and he's got it bad. According to Steven R. Lindsay in *The Handbook of Applied Dog Behavior and Training:*

> PTSD is precipitated by unpredictable life-threatening trauma that may or may not result in actual physical injury. The ordinary symptoms of the disorder in dogs include some or all of the following: (1) increased sensitivity to startle (hyper-vigilance) and exhibition of disproportionate levels of generalized or irrational fear; (2) increased irritability and hyper-reactivity; (3) a tendency to behave in impulsive and explosive ways in association with increased affective liability (mood swings); (4) the presence of hyperactivity; (5) a tendency to behave aggressively under minimal provocation; (6) a strong tendency toward social isolation and avoidance; (7) a lack of normal sensitivity to pleasure and pain (anhedonia) or numbing; and (8) depressed mood.

Hmm, sounds familiar. Let's look at Lava a little more closely, shall we, and examine which (or, more accurately, how many) of these symptoms he exhibits on a regular basis. He's got the opener, "unpredictable life-threatening trauma," covered: Fallujah, combat zone, shooting, bombs, even a near-fatal run-in with a Land Rover in the suburbs of La Jolla.

And I've already mentioned some of Lava's overprotective behavior and his tendency to go berserk when he hears the FedEx truck coming up the street. But let's take each of the above points individually and determine its merit when placed in the context of Lava's behavior:

1. Increased sensitivity to startle/disproportionate levels of generalized or irrational fear: Lava most certainly displays these traits on a near-daily basis. The UPS driver within the vicinity of our front door? Lava is going absolutely ape-shit, barking, hair up on his neck, all of that. He is hyper-vigilant and prone to overprotectiveness and has what I feel is a completely irrational fear of the ocean. He trembles at the prospect of being within two hundred yards of the ocean—not ideal considering where we live. It's really not that much of a stretch to imagine where his fear originated, but I keep thinking he'll realize it's just water.

2. Increased irritability and hyper-reactivity: The most innocuous and routine occurrences—children calling to one another at the park—can turn Lava into a stark raving lunatic. Enough said.

3. A tendency to behave in impulsive and explosive ways in association with increased affective liability (mood swings): I've observed Lava on numerous occasions when he's relaxed and napping on the floor or my stepson's bed. Life's a bowl of cherries, right? Wrong. Without warning or apparent provocation, he's going ballistic. Why? What's causing this? Who knows what evil lurks in the mind of Lava? What demons are still there? For example, Lava will be lying on the living room floor, at peace, it would seem, and one of Sean's friends knocks on the door. Innocent enough, you'd think. But Lava goes stark raving berserk. Is he reliving the experience of hearing someone knock on a door just before an RPG hit the building where he was living? I don't know what triggers these reactions, but I can assure you they're very unsettling, and it's all I can do to calm him.

4. The presence of hyperactivity: Hyper? Who? Lava?

5. A tendency to behave aggressively under minimal provocation: Would this be Lava running up to the first dog he sees at the park and accosting him for no reason? You and I would be locked away for some of the things Lava's done to other dogs without *any* provocation whatsoever.

The final three symptoms—(6) non-social; (7) no pain, no pleasure; and (8) depression—don't resonate with my view of Lava. He's actually pretty social, he seems to enjoy the pleasures of life (though he's tough as shit, and has a pretty impressive pain threshold), and he's not really depressed per se. But he's still scoring above 50 percent, and considering that just one or two symptoms would be problematic, I think we can safely say he's got PTSD. Like I said, his vet was convinced he needed medication, one that's made for dogs with "high levels of separation anxiety." When I asked if there would be problems for Lava on this medication, the vet replied, "Hey, a few million people can't be wrong." Let's hope he's right.

If you're still not convinced by a dog expert's analysis, let's look at what the Army has to say about PTSD:

> Anyone who has gone through combat or military exposure can develop Post-Traumatic Stress Disorder (PTSD). Anyone who has lived through a traumatic event that caused them to fear for their lives, see horrible things, and feel helpless, can develop PTSD.

So I guess we can check yes to all that. Does he have the symptoms of it? Again, going to the experts, we learn there are four types of symptoms:

1. **Reliving the event (also called reexperiencing symptoms):** *Can be triggered by sight or sound.* Check. The ocean waves crashing on the rocks at the beach take Lava right back to his unhappy place. You'd think he was going to have a seizure on the spot.

2. **Avoiding situations that remind you of it:** Not sure how to measure this with a dog. My guess is that he'd prefer not to spend time in a fifty-five-gallon drum in the middle of incoming enemy fire. He's never said so, but . . . Funny, though, how this is actually the opposite of what many of us Marines might admit. After all, what are we avoiding? War? Most of us have signed up for more than one combat tour, so you can cross that off my list. In fact, even

if a Marine or a grunt or whoever doesn't go back in an official capacity, many return to do other jobs. After all, how can "real life" compare to the excitement of being part of death and destruction day after day?

3. Feeling numb: Lava is anything but numb. That's my absolute favorite thing about Lava. No matter what happens, no matter what is going on, Lava is fully engaged.

4. Feeling keyed up: *Always on the alert and lookout for danger. You can suddenly become angry or irritable, have a hard time sleeping, have trouble concentrating, fear for your safety and always feel on guard, feel very startled when someone surprises you.* They've hit the jackpot here. Check, check, and double check.

When we first got Lava back to the States, he couldn't sit still. He was always on guard, always protecting me. Later, when I started dating my wife, Lava took over protection of her son, Sean. He wouldn't leave his side. When we got married he slept in Sean's bed and continues to do so today. He's even gone after my mother because he thought she was invading the sanctity of Sean's room.

Lava barks at the smallest of noises. He goes crazy when our neighbors leave their house because he thinks they're walking too close to ours. I'm not talking about your garden-variety barking, either. This is a spine-tingling, from-the-gut, wounded-animal howl that he can keep going for what seems an eternity. As Graham describes it, "Lava has the most unbelievably unique bark. It's like a coyote. He uses it to scare people away from him. They always walk away, so that reinforces his behavior and he uses it again and again." It disrupts the entire house. The baby cries, I yell and chase Lava, and my wife gets pissed off like no one's business, as if this entire lunatic episode is my fault. Which, I suppose, it is.

Lava lives to torment more placid dogs at the park, even if they're more than twice his size. For example, he'll introduce his *get-the-fuck-outta-my-way* bark into any dog social that might wind up with a golden retriever coming over to check us out. Lava will leap into the park, make a beeline for a new dog, and is soon barking and bouncing on his front legs as if he's got a hydraulically assisted front end. In a way it's funny to watch, but it can get embarrassing, too, and I often find myself apologizing to some poor schmuck who doesn't know Lava's story and thinks he's Cujo incarnate. Lava simply sees everyone—dogs included—as the enemy and a threat to *yours truly*, his savior and best friend (even if he thinks I'm a moron he can outsmart on most days).

Lava is not just this way with dogs. He can sense fear and trepidation in people, too. One of my best friends, whom I'll call Otis, is not a dog lover by any stretch of the imagination, so when he first met Lava you can imagine it wasn't a meeting of the mutual admiration society. Lava was not particularly gracious when Otis finally came through the door. Next thing I knew, Lava's sitting next to his chair at ramrod attention and actually guarding him. Just like a real protection dog. The moment Otis so much as twitched a finger, Lava curled his lip and emitted a low but very threatening and intimidating growl. I told Otis not to move a muscle while

I pulled Lava from the room. It was almost like a scene from a cartoon where the massive, snarling dog is chasing a person down the street, all the while snapping and growling. For some reason, Otis agreed to try again, and he joined us on a ski vacation with Lava. The trip ended with Otis having to leave the townhouse we'd rented through the ground-floor bedroom window, throwing his luggage in front of him.

By that time, Graham was regularly seeing Lava and seemed to be making progress. He was genuinely interested in helping. I think he wanted to show the world that I wasn't crazy for having brought him back. Graham told me he wanted "the public to see the good in Lava." (I would have settled for just my close friends recognizing this.) The classes, the private training, it all seemed to help a little, but it was as much about training me as training the dog. Lava knew how to push my buttons like the finest of best friends, and I always rose to the occasion. Graham didn't have that problem. He could use physical posturing to show Lava some submission but not too much, and he'd keep his composure at all times.

I decided to check into the idea of medication after Lava "attacked" my friend Mark. It was late one morning and I was walking the dogs. I had my son Mattox (at the time about four months old) in the stroller. Now, if Lava is protective of me, he's insanely protective of my kids. Mark, who has two great dogs as well, began to play with Lava. They were just kind of roughhousing, I guess, but ended up doing so a little too close to the stroller, and that's when it happened: Lava laid into Mark three times in rapid succession, managing to lay back a nice flap of skin on his thumb and putting a couple of puncture wounds in his arm. Fortunately, none of these injuries required sutures, but they were bleeding pretty badly. We walked to my house so I could clean and bandage the wounds for Mark, and I had to put Lava in the garage before Mark could come into our yard. Lava was clearly still agitated and his behavior, unpredictable.

One of the most embarrassing episodes, however, occurred one day in the park. We saw a young couple sitting on a blanket enjoying the warmth of the sun and basking in the beautiful San Diego weather. Everything seemed to be going great. Lava and Koda were playing, chasing each other around the park and seemingly oblivious to the couple on the blanket. All seemed to be idyllic—until Lava happened. You know, like the saying, shit happens? Well, that's how it is with Lava sometimes. He just "happens." He strolled over to the pair on the blanket, pretended to have just a passing interest, and then—as he was walking away—paused. I'm thinking, *Oh shit! Lava, noooooo . . . !* Before I could even utter his name, Lava hiked his leg and peed on their blanket. *Hey, it's my park, and you didn't check with me first to see if you could relax here.* And that's just how it goes.

Lava makes a pretty good case for himself as suffering from something. PTSD? As they say, if it walks like a duck, quacks like a duck, and smells like a duck, chances are . . . Should I take under advisement the army's warning that family and friends can deal with the postwar veteran's anger or violent behavior by going "to a safe place and call[ing] for help right away"? Not sure that would work in Lava's case, unless I wanted to watch him being hauled away by animal control while I huddled behind a tree.

The brochures also suggest that your friends and family learn to communicate better. Certainly a good idea, but Lava's methods of barking and licking his private parts don't translate as well as I'd like. Still, he's somehow always gotten through to me.

Am I ever afraid that he would attack the children? Never. He always, always protects family members. It was love at first sight for my stepson, Sean, when he met Lava. Since my marriage, Lava has slept in Sean's bed every night and never displayed any aggression toward him. In fact, Lava connects with kids in general. Graham has boarded Lava when I've gone out of town, and he has a young son. "Lava was scratching at my son's door one night," Graham says, "and I decided to let him in to see what he wanted. He immediately ran to my son's bed, jumped up, and curled up by his feet. Lava gave a huge sigh of relief, like *Now I can finally relax.*" He also adds, however, that when Lava heard his wife's footsteps in the hall outside the bedroom, he began his low growl. I guess that's what you call high-level resource guarding.

He also took to Cheddar the cat, forming a strong bond across species. So no, I don't worry about Lava and anyone in our house. My mother is another story—Lava will allow her to pet him when she's sitting down, but when she stands or goes into the kids' rooms, he gets very protective of the children.

Lava and I know firsthand how easily life can be taken away if you're not paying vigilant, constant attention. (Even that is not always enough.) So maybe I'm not a "normal" person, especially if Lava and his actions—like being protective of his family, for example—are a reflection of my own. Okay, I don't just arbitrarily assault other people when I see them at the dog park. And as far as I know, I haven't tried to hump anyone in public as a display of my dominance. It's just that from time to time, I still think about the things I saw and experienced during our time in Fallujah. At the risk of repeating myself, I don't think I suffer from PTSD—at least not in the classic sense—but there's something there just beneath the surface that I can't quite put my finger on.

Maybe I owe it to myself and my family to talk to someone more equipped to evaluate my mental health. If I'm suggesting that other people go, maybe I owe it to everyone else to at least check out the couch. Hey, Tony Soprano sucked it up. Maybe I can, too.

CHAPTER NINE

OPENING THE SNIVEL BOOK

"Nobody wants to be that guy who says, 'I got counseling this afternoon, Sergeant,'" he said, mimicking a whining voice.
—FROM AN INTERVIEW WITH AN IRAQ COMBAT VETERAN CONVICTED OF MANSLAUGHTER[13]

When I think about actually making that call to announce that I'm thinking about . . . *therapy* . . . it just makes me want to dry-heave. Every father gets annoyed with his kid at one time or another; does it mean I need therapy? Oh sure, I'm the one who, on duty in Iraq and completely on edge all the time, waiting to be blown up while making a supply run or taking a piss or killing or watching friends be killed, noted in my first book, "It feels normal. Despite the bombs and the insurgents and the rubble, it feels like I belong here." I felt at home in the middle of all the mayhem, death, and destruction that war renders. Does that make me psycho? Crazy? A mumbling vet, packing heat in the middle of a summer's day?

I suppose one incentive to go is that every time I drive past the intersection leading to the VA hospital, I see one or another homeless veteran standing on the corner with a cardboard placard proclaiming his homelessness and hunger and willingness to work for food (but always more than happy to receive a free "Jackson" or "Benjamin" in lieu of same). I am haunted by thoughts of not being able to support my wife and child. The homeless, hungry vet is clearly deranged, in my clinical and professional opinion . . . and he could be me were it not for the love of a dog who, through no planned effort on his part, brought me the love of a woman. In other words, there but for the grace of God go I, babbling and raging into the Western sunset.

I have the goods to talk about. I've seen some stuff. You tell me what you think. How about this: Combat doesn't happen the way *Hollywood* portrays it in the movies. People don't die slowly in my experience. There's no last "Tell my wife/mother I love her" as a soldier closes his eyes and lets his head loll gently to one side.

No, death in combat is usually violent and sudden, and the new dearly departed is lucky if he even has a head from which a final breath can be emitted. In combat, moaning and screaming accompany death. And the injuries—not only the fatal ones—are the most disturbing you'd ever want to see.

One day after a particularly ferocious firefight, in which our one UAH (Up-Armored Humvee) is nearly destroyed and we take three casualties (walking wounded, fortunately), we manage to get to the field aid station where the wounded are brought to be triaged and sorted before being transferred to one of the surgical or trauma units in Fallujah or, if necessary, flown to Baghdad or

Balad. I finish giving our vehicles a good once-over—the gun truck has taken multiple rounds from a 12.7mm heavy machine gun and is out of commission until we can find a replacement windshield—and go to check on our wounded.

One of the Marines from another unit, a kid no more than twenty or twenty-one, is lying on a stretcher, morphine dripping through an IV line into his arm. I squat down beside him to comfort him at least a little bit—he's scared, it's there in his eyes, but he doesn't want it to show—and I can see his wound as I hold his hand and tell him everything will be all right. Where his right thigh quadriceps should be, there's only a cavernous, gaping wound extending the entire width of his thigh down to the bone. It's just a bloody, pulpy mess of muscle, fat and god-only-knows-what-else where a hunk of shrapnel, not much bigger than a small rock, nearly severed his leg. Incredibly, they'll be able to save his leg, and after some physical therapy he'll be up and running. Probably straight back to Iraq or Afghanistan for a second, third, or fourth tour.

I've been to the naval hospital at Bethesda twice to visit our wounded troops. It's amazing that some of these kids are alive considering the severity of their wounds—concave skulls, missing limbs, filleted organs. How can you be entirely the same again after witnessing this? You nearly break down and cry when you visit one of the Marines you sent to Iraq as part of a transition team, and who just two weeks later is a twenty-five-year-old with no legs. His attitude is so unbelievably positive. He can't wait to get fitted with his prostheses so he can be up and running again. But you want to scream because it's so goddamn unfair.

I've begun to look more closely at my own behavior; having kids also made me more aware of how I present myself to the world at large. I don't want to always be looking over my shoulder, expecting to lose everything that's good in my life. That's why I agreed to give therapy a try. I'm also doing it for the good of the people who will read this book—the veterans and their families and friends who might benefit from overcoming all that macho bullshit and getting help. It can't *hurt* anyone to talk, either. Have I convinced you? Lava is laughing his head off at me, so his vote is in.

On January 2, 2008, I call the VA hospital here in San Diego to set up an appointment. Everyone who knows I'm doing this is thrilled. Even though I keep reminding them that I'm a journalist in this situation. Everyone but me, that is. I'm not so thrilled about the prospects of being "in the system," as they say, and even less excited about being referred to something called the Mood Disorder Clinic and having to answer the questions on the Beck Depression Inventory, a survey of twenty-two questions that the head shrinkers use to determine if you're depressed or not. My mind immediately races with thoughts of Xanax, Prozac, mood-altering chemicals—and worse. I picture myself going in as a perfectly functioning normal adult and coming out a veritable zombie after undergoing electroshock convulsion therapy, a black rubber block wedged between my teeth and held in place by a leather strap wound under my chin and over my head, the clamps leading to a car battery attached to my testicles.

They can't get me in for almost a month, so I'll have plenty of time to think about the torture that awaits. But then I get the opportunity to speak with a Navy psychiatrist about some of the work being done for veterans with PTSD. I ask him to recommend good candidates to interview for this book; he gives me a bunch of names—several of whom, he points out, "could provide you with medication should you need it." I don't know why, but that kind of pisses me off. Here I've barely spoken with the man and he's suggesting I need to be on mood stabilizers?

If the VA is wondering why more vets don't call them up for help, maybe they should think about the phrase *mood disorder*. If *disorder* in the medical sense means a disturbance of normal functioning in the body or mind, then does *mood disorder* mean that your mood is not functioning normally? Being disturbed by what we saw in Iraq actually *is* normal, to my thinking. Then again, if I say I'm not disturbed, does *that* mean I have PTSD? It's a lot easier to diagnose my dog.

I'm grumbling about this out loud one morning and Lava just looks at me long and hard. "Hey, buddy," I tell him, "I know you're juiced, but you were just a puppy. You didn't have the training I had. You're a dog. I'm a man. I'm supposed to be able to cope without chemical help." It's pretty ironic that Lava's to some degree responsible for where I am today, and yet anyone would agree that he's ten times more wacko than most creatures, human or canine. I guess instability loves company.

There are a lot of ways to treat PTSD, or generalized anxiety/depression/anger/whatever, stemming from military experience in a combat zone. Many of them are the same things you're supposed to do for a dog with PTSD. Okay, not the talking cure, but the cognitive therapy, where you replace your negative thoughts (human) or actions (dog) with something positive. Or you can purposefully focus on the bad thing that happened (human) or actually relive it in a safe way (dog) so that you become less afraid of that memory. Finally, there are the drugs (human) and the drugs (dog) that can take the edge off and help you use the various therapies out there. I don't want or need medication. Lava had no choice. It's helped him enormously, though. Graham told me that medication has actually saved dogs' lives; without it, they are just too hard to rehabilitate.

The antidepressants that Lava takes are similar to the ones humans use—kind of like Prozac. Perhaps you've heard of it? It's part of a class of drugs called selective serotonin reuptake inhibitors (SSRIs) and I'll tell you, I've seen it in action and it works. Chemicals in your brain can cause you to act in certain ways (anxious, depressed, aggressive) so the thinking is that these drugs can rebalance the chemicals that are out of whack so that you can behave in a more socially acceptable way. There are numerous studies that show these medications help people suffering from full-on PTSD. They've been popular in the States for almost twenty years—for both dog and human.

To Lava's veterinarian, it was a no-brainer. He said he doesn't prescribe it too often, but that with a dog with Lava's background, there were bound to be issues that couldn't be helped by behavior modification alone. The intense separation anxiety and over-protective personality needed an extra boost. The SSRIs are considered incredibly safe. They also give me a chance to try and reassure Lava that he's safe. He can relax and let down his guard, and begin to realize that the mailman isn't delivering anything explosive.

All that said, activity interests me more than medicine, so I'm especially interested in learning about the Virtual Reality

Medical Center (VRMC) in San Diego. Psychiatrists, psychologists, and researchers there use VR as treatment for anxiety and panic disorders, social phobias, and PTSD. The program is currently a pilot (or test) project funded by the Office of Naval Research (ONR). It's pretty wild—they simulate different combat experiences so thoroughly it's like you're really there, but instead of actually being killed by insurgent fire you just *think* you're dead. (Somehow that doesn't sound as cool as it plays. But it works.) You're wearing a headset and all you can see and hear is the simulated scene. The army originally created much of this stuff to train soldiers. Now it's using VR to *re*train us.

If someone comes back with PTSD, reliving the moment when his Humvee was blown up by an improvised explosive device during a convoy can actually make him stop flashing back to the scene, because it allows him to realize that it's not really happening. The sessions are designed to push each individual's trigger, and if things get too intense, or the patient becomes too anxious, they can go somewhere else in the scenario or simply remove the headset. All the while, the subjects are sitting in a controlled environment in the safety of an office here in the United States. It's a little counterintuitive, and it has to be done right, but the results are impressive: More than 90 percent of participants claim to be much more comfortable in their daily activities than before treatment. But it doesn't happen overnight.

If a dog survives being hit by a car and is then scared to death of walking even on a sidewalk alongside the road, you're supposed to gradually sensitize him back to the sound of traffic. If you just shove him by the curb and hold him there, he's only going to become more skittish. You have to go slow and be really supportive. That's what the team at the VRMC do. They recommend eight to twelve sessions. (Don't try treating yourself at home with *Call of Duty 4, Halo 3,* or *Turok* on your Xbox 360. The VR environment was created by recycling virtual graphic assets initially built for the U.S. Army–funded combat tactical simulation scenario, and the Xbox game, *Full Spectrum Warrior.*[14] I kid you not.)

I want to find out more, so I call the first name on the list. Dr. Dennis Wood plays a big role in the VRMC. He's a retired Navy captain, having served a combined reserve and active-duty obligation of thirty-four years, and he does not have the ability to prescribe, so hopefully I'll avoid that issue on day one. In addition to the work he does with the VRMC here in San Diego, he's also a psychologist in private practice in Coronado. He offers to talk to me sooner rather than later. Our initial phone conversation is collegial. We have a great discussion about the wonders of VR as a way to treat veterans diagnosed with or exhibiting PTSD. I explain that I want to do some research for this book; if I find out anything about myself in the process, all the better.

Full disclosure: My publisher got in touch first with Dennis and talked to him about the book. He wasn't that surprised, considering that the large majority of his clients are brought in by their family or friends, or by an enlisted man's commanding officer. Very few veterans of recent wars voluntarily walk into a clinic.

★ ★ ★

My first meeting with Dr. Wood is at the offices of VRMC. They're located in a sprawling office park here in San Diego, not unlike so many other clusters of three-story steel, glass, and concrete buildings housing medical, high-tech, and real estate offices. There's no guard in the lobby, just the directory on the wall, pointing visitors to any number of nondescript doors leading to generic, unpretentious office suites. We meet in a conference room. I'm able to ask Dr. Wood some questions about PTSD and the application of VR to treat it. He enlightens me that afternoon, whetting my appetite for more information and an opportunity to see the system at work.

My curiosity getting the better of me—and because I do have a vested personal interest in finding out—I ask the doctor if there is anything that predisposes a person to suffer PTSD. He tells me that there are indeed indicators:

1. Genetic markers
2. Multiple or single trauma(s) during the developmental years
3. Lack of resilience training (essentially introducing stress-inducing types of events likely to be encountered) during the pre-deployment period (Here Dr. Wood relates to me the history of one sailor diagnosed with PTSD who was assigned to work with Army special forces in Afghanistan and who ultimately saw firsthand horrifying brutality by the Taliban, for which he was not prepared.)
4. Constant arousal. (Not *that* kind, you creeps—say, mortar and rocket shelling.)
5. History of psychological difficulties and/or alcohol or drug abuse, sometimes brought on by post-deployment self-medication to ease the pain
6. Unit cohesion—how accepted does the new guy feel? For women, sexual harassment or not being perceived as integral to success in combat makes for particular susceptibility to PTSD.

It's funny, but by these markers, Lava's personality doesn't seem such a PTSD slam-dunk. Then again, Lava's trainer, Graham, mentioned genetic markers, too, and pointed out that Lava was not exactly the product of an AKA-certified stud. Chances are that his father, and a few fathers before him, were essentially feral.

Following our conversation, Dr. Wood takes me around the offices of VRMC to introduce me to some people, including the founder, Mark Wiederhold, M.D., Ph.D. The offices are unremarkable—they could belong to any number of businesses, from an erectile dysfunction treatment clinic to a penny-stock boiler-room operation—except the work being done here is infinitely more important to society.

Then it's time to see the VR room. It's not the full-blown dog-and-pony show I hoped for, because the equipment and manpower to monitor my reactions aren't available, but it's interesting to see and experience the scenarios nonetheless.

The computer software is very realistic, and as I go through the scenarios—a grunt on the ground searching out bad guys; a turret gunner in a convoy complete with an insurgent technical (a pickup truck with a machine gun in the back); an observer in a virtual Fallujah—I try to monitor myself for the markers the technicians and psychologists use to monitor a patient's progress or levels of anxiety: elevated respiratory and heart rates (levels of arousal).

Had I been hooked up, Dr. Wood would have been able to accurately monitor my respiration, heart rate, peripheral temperature (finger temperature, which is normal at around ninety-two degrees Fahrenheit and drops when the fight-or-flight instinct kicks in), and galvanic skin response (sweaty palms), which is graded on a scale of one through ten, one being normal. These inputs are used to give the clinician an indication of the level of anxiety a patient is experiencing at any time and allow him or her to talk the patient down.

The patient can then practice any of the relaxation techniques he is taught or simply remove the VR headset. One of the relaxation techniques Dr. Wood describes is the "*Happy Gilmore* happy place." That is, you imagine yourself in a situation that brings you comfort and safety, as Adam Sandler's character did to calm his nerves on the golf course in the movie *Happy Gilmore*.

Dr. Wood and his team published an article about their success thus far, although it's still quite new. All six of the patients treated reported less anxiety and depression after ten sessions in the program.[15]

The potential for VR in PTSD prevention and treatment is really unlimited. The problem lies in getting warriors to use it. And there's the rub. An example of what the military has traditionally done to assess Marines' or soldiers' likelihood of developing PTSD following a combat deployment is to give them those PDHAs to fill out, seeking answers to questions such as where they were deployed; their assessment of their own emotional health; their exposure to combat, specifically blast or explosion, vehicle accident, and fragment wound above the shoulders (all checking for a possible traumatic brain injury, or TBI); whether or not they saw dead bodies; and if they ever felt in danger for their lives. What? It's combat these folks are in. If they didn't feel in danger for their lives, I'd have to really wonder.

Here's what happens, though. Marines, soldiers, and sailors fill in this assessment in Iraq or Kuwait immediately before coming home. These kids have been looking forward to coming home since they got on the plane to deploy. But wait. Here comes the good part: The box containing all the PDHAs is lost. The warriors come home and plan to spend a few days away from the unit in the loving embrace of their families. Not so fast, bucko! You don't go anywhere until the PDHAs have been completed. So you sit in a set of bleachers with a staff sergeant or gunnery sergeant yelling at you to hurry up, and oh by the way, you'd better not answer yes to any of the tough questions or no one goes anywhere. Get the picture?

Despite the possibility of things going undetected with this system, the numbers are staggering. Of the Marines in Iraq, the following reported percentages reflect their combat experiences:

95 percent attacked or ambushed

92 percent received incoming artillery, rocket, or mortar fire

97 percent shot at or received small-arms fire

87 percent shot or directed fire at the enemy

65 percent responsible for the death of an enemy combatant

28 percent responsible for the death of a noncombatant

94 percent saw dead bodies or human remains

And the relationship between Marines' combat experience and PTSD is clear with the support of even more overwhelming numbers. Of deployed soldiers and Marines, the prevalence of PTSD increased with the number of firefights; 4.5 per cent for no firefights, 9.3 per cent for one to two firefights, 12.7 percent for three to five firefights, and 19.3 per cent for more than five firefights.[16]

If the DoD had the sense to use VR—specifically the scenarios currently being used by VRMC to assess our warriors—then we could virtually forgo the use of the PDHA and more accurately determine an individual's susceptibility to PTSD. Treatment could begin immediately. We could train our heroes to modify their behavior in order to live happier and more fulfilled lives as civilians before it's too late.

LTC Kopelman,

I was deployed to Iraq as a civilian contract fire
lieutenant from August 2004 to August 2005, spending
the first 8 months at Logistical Support Area (LSA)
Anaconda in Balad.

   While I was at Anaconda I discovered a black dog
living outside of the security fence. "Black Dog"
was a stray, literally living under one of the guard
towers outside of the wire. I am pretty sure that
the soldiers in the tower were feeding the dog on
a regular basis, and of course we would often stop
on our way back to the fire house from the dining
facility and heave some leftovers to Black Dog. I
also had some family and friends send me some large
dog chew bones in my care packages. I would send the
chew bones up to the guards in the tower and they
would give Black Dog these treats from the States.

   I knew of a National Guard unit who had rescued
two stray dogs from LSA
Anaconda, so naturally
I thought I might be
able to do the same for
Black Dog. Any rescue
would be a long shot
because unlike Miss
Sippy and Rex, who
both lived on the base
and were rescued by a
Mississippi National
Guard unit, Black Dog
lived outside of the

"Black Dog" outside the fence of Camp
Anaconda in Balad, Iraq

wire and had never been socialized with humans. His
only interaction was by the food that dropped out of
the sky from the guard tower.

My plan was to have the Quick Reaction Force pick
up the dog, take him to the installation vet for a
quick physical, and then fly him to Kuwait on an
army aircraft. Although I had talked to most of the
parties who would be involved in the rescue, my plan
hit a snag when our entire civilian fire department
was shipped to another army base in Iraq. Before I
left, I took a few pictures of Black Dog and bid him
farewell.

Hopefully, Black Dog is still living under the
tower on a diet of DFAC food supplied by the soldiers
in the tower and other dog lovers.

I was saddened that I could not help Black Dog,
but hearing about soldiers and Marines who were
successful in bringing some kindness and caring to
the many Iraqi dogs (and cats) warms my heart. Thank
you for rescuing Lava from a dismal life and thank
you for your service to our country.

Dennis K Donehoo

Dennis Donehoo

CHAPTER TEN

NEVER QUIT

"There was one catch and that was Catch-22. Orr would be crazy to fly more missions and sane if he didn't, but if he was sane he had to fly them. If he flew them he was crazy and didn't have to; but if he didn't want to he was sane and had to."

—JOSEPH HELLER, *CATCH-22*

'**ve learned about the different kinds of therapy,** but I suspect that whatever I do someone is going to ask me about my father. I've made the first call but waiting is no good, so I look again at the list I have. What if these guys are complete dicks? What if they spend their Thursday nights tasting wine in Sonoma? Then what?

My appointment day at the VA Mood Disorder Clinic arrives and naturally I'm apprehensive. I mean, I'm entering uncharted territory here. What will it be like? Will I be in a waiting room with a bunch of drooling, babbling Vietnam-era veterans, wearing their field jackets with all the patches on them à la *The Deer Hunter*? Adding to my newfound anxiety is the fact that parking is abysmal.

I drive around the VA lot (angrily, of course) for twenty minutes, which makes me late, which fuels my anxiety. *Fuck, fuck, fuck all to hell!*

When I finally get to Second Floor North (where the outpatient loonies wait for their appointments) to sign in, I notice a rather full waiting room, which suggests to me that there are a whole slew of vets in need of help. This doesn't bode well for the young kids who will one day come home from Iraq and Afghanistan markedly different from the carefree twenty-somethings they were before they went to war.

Going to your therapist is different from going to the regular doctor. They don't take your vital signs—I guess it wouldn't tell them anything. You can appear to be calm and centered with a low, steady pulse, but if you're ready for a straitjacket and a room with padded walls you could crack at a moment's notice. No, temperature and blood pressure aren't being checked this day. You sign in at a desk as usual, and you sit and wait as usual, but the nurses and administrative staff who go about their daily business don't look at you like you're just there for a routine appointment. This look is more guarded, almost pitying. Like, *Wow, you poor bastard, I feel so bad for you with what you must have going on in your scrambled-up head. And it's a shame, too, because you don't really* look *deranged or anything. In fact, you're kind of attractive, and I might even talk to you under other circumstances, but we all know why you're here, so please don't even glance at me.*

So I sign in, sit and read my book—*Jarhead* (what else?)— and wait to meet with my caseworker. He's a very nice gentleman who's been working at the VA for thirty-six years. (I know this because I feel it my obligation to interview him as much as he plans to interview me, and because I want to know my health care providers' credentials.) He either loves what he does or he gets some kind of perverse pleasure from hanging out around a bunch of nut jobs.

Hell, after thirty-six years of doing psychological inventories and writing evaluations, who's to say he's not completely wacked out himself, right? Oh yeah, these people who deal with the mumblers, screamers, and loonies every day, they try their best to treat you like anyone else they meet at a cocktail party, but there's this look they get when you tell them everything's really okay, that you're really just trying to do some research for your book.

That look of impending doom, that they know what a wack job you really are because only the true nuts and loons say everything is okay and they're really just doing book research when in reality (which gets very twisted and turned upside down) you're the biggest psycho since McMurphy in Ken Kesey's *One Flew Over the Cuckoo's Nest,* and you're about to say, "I'm here to cooperate with ya a hundred percent. A hundred percent. I'll be just right down the line with ya, you watch. 'Cause I think we ought to get to the bottom of R. P. McMurphy." Or, in this case, Jay Kopelman.

There's nothing comfortable or comforting about the questions I'm asked: "How's your relationship with your wife?" "How do you get along with your stepson?" "How does your obsessive-compulsiveness manifest itself?" "When did you first notice that you were having anger-management issues?" "Were you abused as a child?" "Were you ever sexually molested?" "Was your father nurturing?"

Hey, isn't that the mother's job? I want to scream.

There's nothing fun at all about having your psyche probed with questions about abuse, molestation, and your father's ability (or lack thereof) to nurture. What have I gotten myself into? I thought this would be more about my military career. You know, "Why did you join up?" "What did you hope to accomplish in Iraq?" "Was there anything you did that you really didn't want to do?" "Is there one incident that stands out in your mind?" I fully expected the "How did that make you feel" after each of my responses. But this personal stuff? What a fucking disaster.

So we have this conversation, the social worker and me. We talk of family and personal interests. I tell him that I'm a competitive cyclist and he tells me he has a son who's a competitive triathlete. We talk about tennis and the Australian Open and who we each think will win, shit like that. He then asks me if I have any questions before we part. "Uh, yeah, I was wondering, so what do you think? I mean, am I nuts, or what?"

"No, I think you're a perfectly normal, healthy adult," he replies.

Uh-huh. *Why don't I believe you?* He tells me that they're going to call me to arrange five sessions. Yeah, right. More like five weeks' accommodations at the Ha-Ha Hotel. You check in, but you never check out—at least not as the same person you were when you voluntarily subjected yourself to the scrutiny of modern mind bending.

I get a call a few days later to schedule an appointment with a therapist—a social worker, actually, with a master's degree and some psychology background—who's good, I guess, at helping you modify behaviors that may be problematic if you're interested in staying married or having a good relationship with your children.

I know the day is coming, and I try to play it down by saying things to people I know like, "Yeah, my publisher wants me to go to this therapy thing so I can write about it, but there's really nothing wrong with me and I'll check it out and see what's going on so *other* people—people with *real* problems—will be helped by what I learn. I mean, I don't have any real issues, but those other people . . ." Man, do I have a lot to learn.

I get to the VA hospital for my appointment, and instead of going to the waiting room with all the normal loonies I have to go to the other end of the cuckoo floor. The end of the floor where the *real* crazies hang out. If this weren't so, there wouldn't be steel doors keeping everyone behind on constant lockdown.

This is when it hits me that someone, somewhere, thinks I am completely over-the-top stark raving mad. Why else would I be in this area with the controlled access? Only I'm confused because I don't hear the wailing, moaning, and ranting I expected. Maybe it's because they keep the patients so sedated they're incapable of any of the inherent maniacal behavior depicted in movies like *A Beautiful Mind*. No, there is no screaming, no steroid-infused orderlies running to restrain the violently delusional (at least not that I can see, but I know they're lurking just around the corner). There's only calm and quiet, and this is as unsettling to me as anything I expected to encounter.

My therapist is a very nice woman, with that look that's a mix of understanding and pity. Add in the practiced air of calm and serenity and not only do you feel comfortable about opening up, but you're ready to say things you'd never admit to anyone.

But I can't shake this feeling that the therapist is a scientist working with a bunch of wild monkeys. As long as she stays calm, the monkeys won't go completely ape-shit, thereby necessitating a call to the orderlies. I don't want to be the bad monkey. No one knows exactly where I am, and as long as my therapist (whom I'll call Sigmund even though she's a woman), holds the keys—literally and figuratively—that will allow me to escape lockdown, I'm gonna be the good, calm, and cooperative monkey.

So in Sigmund's office we get to the nitty-gritty of why I'm here. "No, I don't have PTSD," I tell her. "I'm doing research for my new book. My publisher thought it would be good for me to write a chapter about therapy so that other people—you know, people who really need help, but are afraid to ask—will see that if a lieutenant colonel is going, it must be okay." Leadership from the front, right?

"Well, Jay, is it safe to say that even though you're doing research for a book, maybe it would be possible that you're also here to help with some things you have going on? That you will be able to get some information for your book, but we can work on some things for you, too?" She says this in a voice so syrupy sweet that all I can think about is pancakes and French toast.

Huh? "Uh, sure, that sounds good. I mean, I would like to learn to be a better husband and father."

"What do you mean, Jay?"

And that's when it starts. That's when you tell a complete stranger that you're a control freak, have anger-management issues, and cannot fathom for one second where anyone gets this sense of entitlement so prevalent in the civilian world. The questions about parents and childhood really start flying:

"Were your parents angry?"

"How angry?"

"How did that make you feel?"

"Were you ever afraid when you got in trouble as a child?" Answers: "Sometimes." "Very." "I don't know." "No. What is there to be afraid of? A spanking? Big deal. No, I think some of my behavior is learned, though, from watching my parents, you know. I mean, if they could argue and yell, then that must be the way it's done, right?"

No answer from Sigmund. So you keep talking, then suddenly you realize that's what they want. They want you to divulge your secrets, like you pissed your pants as a child when you got yelled at and that will explain everything. Only you realize that if that's what they want it's not what you're going to give them. So you shut up and sit back and wait. (And, no, I didn't piss my pants when I got yelled at. Wouldn't you love to read that?)

But your silence only brings on more silence. Sigmund is practiced at this. I'm sure she's seen it before and she can sit and say nothing probably longer than I can, and the clock is ticking and I'm beginning to realize some things, and so I break. Beat me, freeze me, starve me, I ain't saying shit. But sit there in therapy across a desk from me with your yap closed and giving nothing until I give something first, and I'm like a frigging canary. I won't shut up. Why? What the hell is happening to me?

I want to ask her if I'm telling her what she really wants to know. What everyone who talks to me about the war wants to know. *Did you kill anyone?* In my first book, I hinted at it, gave a snippet about finding a baby in the rubble, but I've never addressed it face-on. Thinking about what I saw, about the war, makes me both exhausted and angry. Mostly it makes me want to concentrate on my beautiful family, which includes a gorgeous baby who will soon learn to walk and talk, a sweet preteen, a smart-as-a-whip beautiful wife who married me despite her father's warning, "It's not easy to be married to a military man." I've always known my father-in-law was smart, and when he's right, he's right. He wasn't even taking into account my out-of-control, barely domesticated dog, fresh from the killing fields of Iraq.

If Lava were a man, no one would even question whether or not he needed to hightail it to the nearest psych ward. Lucky for me, he's not, and I'm his shrink. "Relax on the couch, Lava. Tell me about your father." I have to mock it all, but the truth of the matter is this: Finding that little ball of fur and sharp puppy teeth has taken me on a journey I never expected. All the way to having my head examined. This I can reflect on while I sit with Sigmund. And she's back with more questions.

"Do you like to be in control?" "Does not having control of things frustrate you?" "How does it make you feel when you're not in control?" More answers: "Yes. Hey, I made a twenty-one-year career out of being in control. You had to be in control, and everyone always knew who was in control." "I don't know." "What do you mean? You mean it's okay to feel?" Oh yeah, we're making progress now.

Only, as I sit there and become a little more comfortable in what's happening, I realize that we *are* making progress. That I'm learning things about myself I didn't previously know or wouldn't acknowledge that will help me become a happier, more effective parent and a better, more responsive husband. That this soul-searching, touchy-feely shit isn't so bad after all. That maybe—dare I say it—I *need* this interaction with a professional. Someone who can help me figure it all out.

I won't go into all the dialogue from this first appointment because it might bore you and, yeah, there's some stuff I just don't feel the need to share. Suffice it to say, we did get down to some deep-rooted issues and emotions that needed to see the light of day.

★ ★ ★

The transition from military to civilian life is a difficult one at best. Compound that with having made the military your life for all your adult years—that is, the Marine Corps is the family you've been around the most, and those interpersonal relationships weren't exactly all healthy—then throw in some combat, and what do you have? You've got a bunch of guys and gals who need to figure it all out all over again.

I've lived a fairly martial existence my entire life. My parents were strict, as I've mentioned; my football coaches were screaming lunatics; the Marine Corps gave me more discipline and screaming. Now you go home to live in your communities, where most people are so self-absorbed that they don't even realize anymore that they're on their cell phones while standing in line at the grocery store and talking so loudly you now know things about them you could have easily lived your life without ever learning.

Times have changed, too. What was normal for you as a child—punishment, accepted behavior—is considered barbaric by today's standards. You have to learn to accept the small things, pick your battles, not worry if your kid doesn't always chew with his mouth closed. In the grand scheme of things, it won't make him a better person. Giving him love and understanding and patience will. If the dresser drawer isn't closed that last eighth of an inch, so what? It doesn't mean your wife doesn't love you or care about the house. Be grateful that she's raising the children and doing so with love and compassion so that when they have to deal with the likes of you, they're equipped to do so.

Look, I know I can sound really casual and even mock all this stuff, I'm serious though. It's important to you, your friends, and your families that if you need help you get it.

You may think it's a sign of weakness in character and body. *It's not.* That there's ever been a stigma attached to therapy or to seeking help is wrong. As horrific as the physical wounds are that our warriors receive, it's the emotional trauma that leaves the truly lasting scars. The body is far more capable of healing itself than is the psyche. There are many qualified people to talk to about anything you think you need help with.

Me? I need to be in control, and I have a bad temper. There, I said it. The first and most difficult step is admitting whatever it is you think (or don't think) might be a problem. After that it's pretty easy. In fact, it's downright empowering. That's why I'm going back. That's a promise.

As resistant as I was initially to going, I'm glad I've taken that step. Yeah, it's a real scrotum-punch at first, when you're just getting into it and you worry about what others think. But you know what? Fuck 'em. Because this isn't about anyone else. It's about you. It's about making our warriors whole again and giving them the lives they deserve. The life you deserve.

AFTERWORD

"The time not to become a father is eighteen years
before a war."
—E. B. WHITE

Life is short.

The day Lava was hit by a car served as a sobering
reminder that everything you hold near and dear—no, wait, scratch
that. The day Lava was hit by a car served as a sobering reminder that
everything *I* hold near and dear can be taken from me in the blink of
an eye. It's critical to recognize those people and things that are truly
important in life—those I should hold in the highest esteem and treat
with the utmost respect. Not only am I lucky to have found Lava and
learned the lessons he's taught me, but somehow I also lucked into a
wonderful wife and two amazing children.

The experience of therapy has been . . . well, frankly, unsettling.
I've opened myself up to a complete stranger and answered
questions even Lava knows better than to ask me. If it helps any
of my fellow Marines to realize that *help* is not a four-letter word,
though, it will be worthwhile. I've learned quite a bit about the
collective psyches of our military units, and if the numbers are
right, survival at home is just as critical and uncertain as it is in
the combat zone.

Those numbers show a generation in trouble. Unless more and better ways are found to address the difficulties of multiple long-term deployments and the inherent problems they breed, we'll be facing even higher rates of suicide, divorce, and substance abuse among returning veterans and their families. There is counseling available, and the services offer marital retreats. The Veterans Administration has established the National Center for PTSD, whose goal is to advance the clinical care and social welfare of U.S. veterans through research, education, and training on PTSD and other stress-related disorders. This is all well and good, but until there's a paradigm shift in the military culture—one that will make it okay to have a problem and seek help for it—we will still be faced with a surge in deployment- and combat-related family crises. Every marriage that ends in divorce; every serviceman who kills him- or herself; and every time a young warrior experiences substance abuse issues, we witness a casualty of war.

So what are you going to do about it? Therapy is one way to go, and it's an important option. Researchers have found that many of the Iraq veterans who screen positive for mental health issues don't get the care they need. That's just wrong. Screw the "snivel book" and take advantage of whatever help you're offered. Lava being on antidepressants has made a big difference. He's not doped out and sleeping all the time. He still gets his bark on, but he calms down quicker and listens better. He doesn't seem as stressed as he has been in the past. His vet felt it was the right thing to do, especially in light of his upbringing. Without these meds, lots of problem dogs would be put to sleep by their owners because they're simply too difficult to deal with anymore. So don't knock it.

As has probably become clear, I often look to Lava for answers. Dogs are special in that they seem to have emotions much like those of humans, yet don't worry about what others think about them and their behavior. They rarely hold back. I don't necessarily like, but am almost always amused by, Lava's ability and desire to bark at anyone and everyone he sees coming by, as if to say, *Hey, world, this is my house/park/car, and if you don't like it you don't have to live in it. In fact, I don't want you to want to live in it.*

Lava truly enjoys every moment of life with glee, if not a modicum of insouciance.

Observations of Lava:

1. Bark at whomever you want, whenever you want, for any reason or no reason whatsoever.
2. Pee where the other guy (or gal) just peed.
3. Live every day as if it's your last.
4. You're always the smartest guy in the room if you don't compare yourself.
5. Disobey everything you're told to do.
6. Drink from a toilet. Hey, water's water, after all. (Lava's never really done this one, but I think he'd secretly like to try.)

It's how you comport yourself and what you do for others in life that really matters. It's the capacity to give—and to receive great joy in doing so—that ultimately gives us happiness. My advice to you is to live your life with all the gusto and pleasure of a dog. Specifically, my dog Lava. I'm not suggesting you crap on your neighbor's lawn, but try to enjoy the simple things in life. Find joy and happiness in just lying on your back in the grass while the sun's rays warm you to your core. Hell, howl at the moon if you want. The true measure of the man on Judgment Day is how he lived his life. I consider these things and I ask myself these questions: Did I live life with dignity, modesty, and compassion for others? Have I lived a full life and shared it with others, receiving love in return? Have I found pleasure in the simple things and the wonders of nature? If at the end of the day I can answer *yes* to these questions, then I've lived a full life.

I've talked about how taking care of Lava has served as a focus for me, taking me out of my memories and keeping me firmly in the present. It's also allowed me to build something of a career out of helping Lava by having him—directly and indirectly—help others. I donate portions of my book sales to charities that benefit veterans and their families. I use Lava's name recognition to bring awareness to causes that I think are important and that require attention, and to raise money for animal rescue and training organizations. I also travel around the country, telling Lava's story and lecturing on leadership, the war on terror, and other topics. I'm even starting my own charitable foundation, The Lava Fund, to assist veterans who suffer from post-traumatic stress disorder. To help fund this foundation, I'm starting a number of businesses, a portion of the proceeds of which will go directly to The Lava Fund. I'm focusing on the things I love to do and going from there.

Lastly, I find my greatest distraction from the painful memories of Iraq in my family. My wife, Pam, is my rock and my salvation and I love her deeply. My stepson, Sean, is a wonderful young man of whom I'm immensely proud; I'm thankful to have him in my life. Whether I'm watching him excel at soccer, ace a test, create a new cartoon, ski a black-diamond run, or drop on a wave that's only waist-high to me but over his head, I'm filled with happiness that I get to see the look of pride and accomplishment on his face.

And my son Mattox has given me a gift I never thought existed: unconditional love at first sight. It does exist. As I write this, he's just turned one year old. I hold him and everything else in the world vanishes. It's just the two of us. There's no way to adequately describe the feelings you have when you're holding a twenty-pound bundle of innocence, happiness, and potential. All cares and worries evaporate. My only thoughts at these times are how to protect him; how to provide him with a happy, healthy life; how to become a better man and father for him to emulate. I know he'll be his own man one day, but I need to be the example that will help him become a thoughtful and trusted leader, friend, and father in his own right. The possibilities are endless for Mattox, and when I hold him they are for me, too.

ACKNOWLEDG-MENTS

It might seem odd to begin a book acknowledgment by thanking a dog for anything, but this is what I feel compelled to do. If not for Lava and his constant antics and *joie de vivre* (which is a nice way of saying wild and irascible behavior), there would most certainly be no book to write. I am grateful for his companionship when there were no other companions and for his constant loyalty.

That said, I would like to thank Dennis Wood, Ph.D., for his insight into, and willingness to discuss, post-traumatic stress disorder and the work he and others are doing to combat it through the use of virtual reality. To that end, I want to thank and acknowledge all those involved in the virtual reality project at the Virtual Reality Medical Center in San Diego.

I want to thank my parents for their support and love throughout the victories and defeats of my life. It didn't matter to them whether or not I won or lost—I was always their son.

Thanks also to my agent, Julie Castiglia—though you are often critical (and occasionally contrarian), I'd be nowhere as an author without your guidance and support. Thank you for your grace, counsel, and confidence in my abilities.

I am grateful to Tony Lyons and everyone at Skyhorse Publishing, especially my editor, Ann Treistman, who is as understanding as she is talented, and who believed in this book from its inception. Thank you for your guiding hand, for your sensitivity, and for providing impetus when I needed it most. It was a pleasure working with you again.

To my boys, Mattox and Sean, know that I love you very much and appreciate you every minute of every day. Lastly, thank you to my lovely wife, Pam, for being my best friend, partner, de facto La Jolla editor, and most ardent supporter. Thank you for your patience, love, and understanding (even on my worst days). You make our house a home, and you are the glue that holds us all together. I love you very much.

APPENDICES

I'm including some of the forms and studies that I cite in the book.

1. Post-Deployment Health Assessment (PDHA)
   The form soldiers are asked to complete on returning from active duty.
2. Post-Deployment Health Re-Assessments (PDHRA)
   The form soldiers are asked to complete three to six months after returning from active duty.
3. "Mental Health Needs of Soldiers Increase Several Months After Returning from Iraq War"
   A press release describing findings in the 2007 study published in the *Journal of the American Medical Association*.
4. "An Achievable Vision"
   A summary of the highly-cited Pentagon Report on mental health and the Armed Forces.
5. "Combat Duty in Iraq and Afghanistan, Mental Health Problems, and Barriers to Care"
   The seminal report on the mental health of members of the Army and Marine Corps involved in combat operations in Iraq and Afghanistan, published in 2004.

FROM BAGHDAD TO AMERICA

This form must be completed electronically. Handwritten forms will not be accepted.

POST-DEPLOYMENT HEALTH ASSESSMENT (PDHA)

PRIVACY ACT STATEMENT

AUTHORITY: 10 U.S.C. 136, 1074f, 3013, 5013, 8013 and E.O. 9397.

PRINCIPAL PURPOSE(S): To assess your state of health after deployment in support of military operations and to assist military healthcare providers in identifying and providing present and future medical care you may need. The information you provide may result in a referral for additional healthcare that may include medical, dental or behavioral healthcare or diverse community support services.

ROUTINE USE(S): In addition to those disclosures generally permitted under 5 U.S.C. 552a(b) of the Privacy Act, to other Federal and State agencies and civilian healthcare providers, as necessary, in order to provide necessary medical care and treatment. Responses may be used to guide possible referrals.

DISCLOSURE: Voluntary. If not provided, healthcare WILL BE furnished, but comprehensive care may not be possible.

INSTRUCTIONS: Please read each question completely and carefully before entering your response or marking your selection. YOU ARE ENCOURAGED TO ANSWER EACH QUESTION. ANSWERING THESE QUESTIONS WILL NOT DELAY YOUR RETURN HOME. Withholding or providing inaccurate information may impair a healthcare provider's ability to identify health problems and refer you to appropriate sources for additional evaluation or treatment. If you do not understand a question, please ask for help.

DEMOGRAPHICS

SAMPLE

Last Name ___ First Name ___ Middle Initial ___

Social Security Number ___ Today's Date (dd/mmm/yyyy) ___

Name of Your Unit during this Deployment ___ Date of Birth (dd/mmm/yyyy) ___ Gender ○ Male ○ Female

Service Branch
○ Air Force
○ Army
○ Coast Guard
○ Marine Corps
○ Navy
○ GS Employee
○ Other

Component
○ Active Duty
○ National Guard
○ Reserves
○ Civilian Government Employee
○ Other

Pay Grade
○ E1 ○ O1 ○ W1
○ E2 ○ O2 ○ W2
○ E3 ○ O3 ○ W3
○ E4 ○ O4 ○ W4
○ E5 ○ O5 ○ W5
○ E6 ○ O6
○ E7 ○ O7 ○ Other
○ E8 ○ O8
○ E9 ○ O9
      ○ O10

Date of arrival in theater (dd/mmm/yyyy) ___

Date of departure from theater (dd/mmm/yyyy) ___ Name of Operation: ___

Location of Operation. To what areas were you mainly deployed (land-based operations for more than 30 days)? (Please mark all that apply, including the number of months spent at each location.)
○ Country 1 ___ Time at location (months) ___
○ Country 2 ___ Time at location (months) ___
○ Country 3 ___ Time at location (months) ___
○ Country 4 ___ Time at location (months) ___
○ Country 5 ___ Time at location (months) ___

Occupational specialty during this deployment (MOS/AOC, NEC/NOBC, or AFSC): ___

Combat specialty: ___

Current Contact Information:
Phone: ___
Cell: ___
DSN: ___
Email: ___
Address: ___

Point of Contact who can always reach you:
Name: ___
Phone: ___
Email: ___
Mailing Address: ___

DD FORM 2796, JAN 2008 PREVIOUS EDITION IS OBSOLETE. Page 1 of 7 Pages Adobe Professional 7.0

158

This form must be completed electronically. Handwritten forms will not be accepted.

Service Member's Social Security Number:

1. **Overall, how would you rate your health during the PAST MONTH?**
   - ○ Excellent
   - ○ Very Good
   - ○ Good
   - ○ Fair
   - ○ Poor

2. **Compared to before this deployment, how would you rate your health in general now?**
   - ○ Much better now than before I deployed
   - ○ Somewhat better now than before I deployed
   - ○ About the same as before I deployed
   - ○ Somewhat worse now than before I deployed
   - ○ Much worse now than before I deployed

3. **During the past 4 weeks, how difficult have physical health problems** *(illness or injury)* **made it for you to do your work or other regular daily activities?**
   - ○ Not difficult at all
   - ○ Somewhat difficult
   - ○ Very difficult
   - ○ Extremely difficult

4. **During the past 4 weeks, how difficult have emotional problems** *(such as feeling depressed or anxious)* **made it for you to do your work, take care of things at home, or get along with other people?**
   - ○ Not difficult at all
   - ○ Somewhat difficult
   - ○ Very difficult
   - ○ Extremely difficult

5. **How many times were you seen by a healthcare provider** *(physician, PA, medic, corpsman, etc.)* **for a medical problem or concern during this deployment?**

6. **Did you have to spend one or more nights in a hospital as a patient during this deployment?**
   - ○ No
   - ○ Yes. Reason/dates:

7. **Were you wounded, injured, assaulted or otherwise hurt during this deployment?**
   - ○ No   ○ Yes

7a. **IF YES, are you still having problems related to this event?**
   - ○ No   ○ Yes   ○ Unsure

8. **For any of the following symptoms, please indicate whether you went to see a healthcare provider** *(physician, PA, medic, corpsman, etc.)*, **were placed on quarters** *(Qtrs)* **or given light/limited duty** *(Profile)*, **and whether you are still bothered by the symptom now.**

Symptom	Sick Call?		Qtrs/Profile?		Still Bothered?		Symptom	Sick Call?		Qtrs/Profile?		Still Bothered?	
	No	Yes	No	Yes	No	Yes		No	Yes	No	Yes	No	Yes
Fever	○	○	○	○	○	○	Dizzy, light headed, passed out	○	○	○	○	○	○
Cough lasting more than 3 weeks	○	○	○	○	○	○	Diarrhea	○	○	○	○	○	○
Trouble breathing	○	○	○	○	○	○	Vomiting	○	○	○	○	○	○
Bad headaches	○	○	○	○	○	○	Frequent indigestion/ heartburn	○	○	○	○	○	○
Generally feeling weak	○	○	○	○	○	○	Problems sleeping or still feeling tired after sleeping	○	○	○	○	○	○
Muscle aches	○	○	○	○	○	○	Trouble concentrating, easily distracted	○	○	○	○	○	○
Swollen, stiff or painful joints	○	○	○	○	○	○	Forgetful or trouble remembering things	○	○	○	○	○	○
Back pain	○	○	○	○	○	○	Hard to make up your mind or make decisions	○	○	○	○	○	○
Numbness or tingling in hands or feet	○	○	○	○	○	○	Increased irritability	○	○	○	○	○	○
Trouble hearing	○	○	○	○	○	○	Skin diseases or rashes	○	○	○	○	○	○
Ringing in the ears	○	○	○	○	○	○	Other *(please list)*:	○	○	○	○	○	○
Watery, red eyes	○	○	○	○	○	○							
Dimming of vision, like the lights were going out	○	○	○	○	○	○							
Chest pain or pressure	○	○	○	○	○	○							

DD FORM 2796, JAN 2008   Page 2 of 7 Pages

This form must be completed electronically. Handwritten forms will not be accepted.

Service Member's Social Security Number:

9.a. During this deployment, did you experience any of the following events? *(Mark all that apply)*

(1) Blast or explosion *(IED, RPG, land mine, grenade, etc.)* ○ No ○ Yes

(2) Vehicular accident/crash *(any vehicle, including aircraft)* ○ No ○ Yes

(3) Fragment wound or bullet wound above your shoulders ○ No ○ Yes

(4) Fall ○ No ○ Yes

(5) Other event *(for example, a sports injury to your head). Describe:* ○ No ○ Yes

_____

9.b. Did any of the following happen to you, or were you told happened to you, IMMEDIATELY after any of the event(s) you just noted in question 9.a.? *(Mark all that apply)*

(1) Lost consciousness or got "knocked out" ○ No ○ Yes

(2) Felt dazed, confused, or "saw stars" ○ No ○ Yes

(3) Didn't remember the event ○ No ○ Yes

(4) Had a concussion ○ No ○ Yes

(5) Had a head injury ○ No ○ Yes

9.c. Did any of the following problems begin or get worse after the event(s) you noted in question 9.a.? *(Mark all that apply)*

(1) Memory problems or lapses ○ No ○ Yes

(2) Balance problems or dizziness ○ No ○ Yes

(3) Ringing in the ears ○ No ○ Yes

(4) Sensitivity to bright light ○ No ○ Yes

(5) Irritability ○ No ○ Yes

(6) Headaches ○ No ○ Yes

(7) Sleep problems ○ No ○ Yes

9.d. In the past week, have you had any of the symptoms you indicated in 9.c.? *(Mark all that apply)*

(1) Memory problems or lapses ○ No ○ Yes

(2) Balance problems or dizziness ○ No ○ Yes

(3) Ringing in the ears ○ No ○ Yes

(4) Sensitivity to bright light ○ No ○ Yes

(5) Irritability ○ No ○ Yes

(6) Headaches ○ No ○ Yes

(7) Sleep problems ○ No ○ Yes

10. Did you encounter dead bodies or see people killed or wounded during this deployment? *(Mark all that apply)*
○ No ○ Yes (○ Enemy ○ Coalition ○ Civilian)

11. Were you engaged in direct combat where you discharged a weapon?
○ No ○ Yes (○ land ○ sea ○ air)

12. During this deployment, did you ever feel that you were in great danger of being killed?
○ No ○ Yes

13. Have you ever had any experience that was so frightening, horrible, or upsetting that, IN THE PAST MONTH, you ....

a. Have had nightmares about it or thought about it when you did not want to? ○ No ○ Yes

b. Tried hard not to think about it or went out of your way to avoid situations that remind you of it? ○ No ○ Yes

c. Were constantly on guard, watchful, or easily startled? ○ No ○ Yes

d. Felt numb or detached from others, activities, or your surroundings? ○ No ○ Yes

14. Over the PAST MONTH, have you been bothered by the following problems?

	Not at all	Few or several days	More than half the days	Nearly every day
a. Little interest or pleasure in doing things	○	○	○	○
b. Feeling down, depressed, or hopeless	○	○	○	○

15. Alcohol is occasionally available during deployments, e.g., R&R, port call, etc. Prior to deploying or during this deployment:

a. Did you use alcohol more than you meant to? ○ No ○ Yes

b. Have you felt that you wanted to or needed to cut down on your drinking? ○ No ○ Yes

c. How often do you have a drink containing alcohol?
○ Never ○ Monthly or less ○ 2 to 4 times a month ○ 2 to 3 times a week ○ 4 or more times a week

d. How many drinks containing alcohol do you have on a typical day when you are drinking?
○ 1 or 2 ○ 3 or 4 ○ 5 or 6 ○ 7 to 9 ○ 10 or more

e. How often do you have six or more drinks on one occasion?
○ Never ○ Less than monthly ○ Monthly ○ Weekly ○ Daily

DD FORM 2796, JAN 2008　　　　　　　　　　　　　Page 3 of 7 Pages

This form must be completed electronically. Handwritten forms will not be accepted.

Service Member's Social Security Number: _____

16. Are you worried about your health because you were exposed to: *(Mark all that apply)*	No	Yes
Animal bites	O	O
Animal bodies *(dead)*	O	O
Chlorine gas	O	O
Depleted uranium *(If yes, explain)* _____	O	O
Excessive vibration	O	O
Fog oils (smoke screen	O	O
Garbage	O	O
Human blood, body fluids, body parts, or dead bodies	O	O
Industrial pollution	O	O
Insect bites	O	O
Ionizing radiation	O	O
JP8 or other fuels	O	O
Lasers	O	O
Loud noises	O	O
Paints	O	O
Pesticides	O	O
Radar/Microwaves	O	O
Sand/dust	O	O
Smoke from burning trash or feces	O	O
Smoke from oil fire	O	O
Solvents	O	O
Tent heater smoke	O	O
Vehicle or truck exhaust fumes	O	O
Other exposures to toxic chemicals or materials, such as ammonia, nitric acid, etc.: *(If yes, explain)* _____	O	O

17. **Were you exposed to any chemicals or other hazard** *(industrial, environmental, etc.)* **that required you to seek immediate medical care?**
   O No   O Yes

18. **Did you enter or closely inspect any destroyed military vehicles?**
   O No   O Yes

19. **Do you think you were exposed to any chemical, biological, or radiological warfare agents during this deployment?**
   O No   O Don't know   O Yes, explain with date and location _____

20. **This question assesses your personal risk for exposure to tuberculosis or other local infectious diseases.**
   Would you say your INDOOR contact with local or 3rd country nationals was:
   O None   O Minimal   O Moderate   O Extensive
              (less than 1 hour per week)   *(1 or more hours per week, but not daily)*   *(at least 1 hour per day, every day)*

21. **Force Health Protection Measures. Please indicate which of the following items you used during this deployment and how often you used them.**

	Daily	Most days	Some days	Never	Not available	Not required
DEET insect repellent applied to skin	O	O	O	O	O	O
Pesticide-treated uniforms	O	O	O	O	O	O
Eye protection *(not commercial sunglasses or prescription glasses)*	O	O	O	O	O	O
Hearing protection	O	O	O	O	O	O
N-95 or other respirator *(not gas mask)*	O	O	O	O	O	O
Pills to stay awake, like dexedrine	O	O	O	O	O	O
Anti-NBC meds	O	O	O	O	O	O
Pyridostigmine *(nerve agent pill)*	O	O	O	O	O	O
Nerve agent antidote injector	O	O	O	O	O	O
Seizure/convulsion antidote injector	O	O	O	O	O	O
NBC gas mask	O	O	O	O	O	O
MOPP over garments	O	O	O	O	O	O

DD FORM 2796, JAN 2008   Page 4 of 7 Pages

FROM BAGHDAD TO AMERICA

This form must be completed electronically. Handwritten forms will not be accepted.

Service Member's Social Security Number: _____

22. Did you receive any vaccinations just before or during this deployment?
- ○ Smallpox *(leaves a scar on the arm)*
- ○ Anthrax
- ○ Botulism
- ○ Typhoid
- ○ Meningococcal
- ○ Yellow Fever
- ○ Other, list: _____
- ○ No
- ○ Don't know

23. Were you told to take medicines to prevent malaria?
○ No   ○ Yes

If YES, please indicate which medicines you took and whether you missed any doses. *(Mark all that apply)*

Anti-malarial medications	Took All Pills
○ Chloroquine (Aralen®)	○ No ○ Yes
○ Doxycycline (Vibramycin®)	○ No ○ Yes
○ Mefloquine (Lariam®)	○ No ○ Yes
○ Primaquine	○ No ○ Yes
○ Other :	○ No ○ Yes

24. Would you like to schedule a visit with a healthcare provider to further discuss your health concern(s)?   ○ No   ○ Yes

25. Are you currently interested in receiving information or assistance for a stress, emotional or alcohol concern?   ○ No   ○ Yes

26. Are you currently interested in receiving assistance for a family or relationship concern?   ○ No   ○ Yes

27. Would you like to schedule a visit with a chaplain or a community support counselor?   ○ No   ○ Yes

S A M P L E

DD FORM 2796, JAN 2008   Page 5 of 7 Pages

162

APPENDICES

This form must be completed electronically. Handwritten forms will not be accepted.

Service Member's Social Security Number: _____

Health Care Provider Only
Post-Deployment Health Care Provider Review, Interview, and Assessment

1. Do you have any medical or dental problems that developed during this deployment?   ○ Yes   ○ No
   If yes, are the problems still bothering you now?   ○ Yes   ○ No

2. Are you currently on a profile (or LIMDU) that restricts your activities (light or limited duty)?   ○ Yes   ○ No

   If yes: For what reason? _____   ○ NA

   Is your condition due to an injury or illness that occurred during the deployment?   ○ Yes   ○ No   ○ NA
   Did you have similar problems prior to deployment?   ○ Yes   ○ No   ○ NA
   If so, did your condition worsen during the deployment?   ○ Yes   ○ No   ○ NA

3. Ask the following behavioral risk questions. Conduct risk assessment as necessary.

   a. Over the PAST MONTH, have you been bothered by thoughts that you would be better off dead or of hurting yourself in some way?   ○ Yes   ○ No

   IF YES, about how often have you been bothered by these thoughts?   ○ A few days   ○ More than half of the time   ○ Nearly every day

   b. Over the PAST MONTH, have you had thoughts or concerns that you might hurt or lose control with someone?   ○ Yes   ○ No   ○ Unsure

4. If member reports YES or UNSURE responses to 3.a. or 3.b., conduct risk assessment.

   a. Does member pose a current risk for harm to self or others?   ○ No, not a current risk   ○ Yes, poses a current risk   ○ Unsure

   b. Outcome of assessment   ○ Immediate referral   ○ Routine follow-up referral   ○ Referral not indicated

5. Alcohol screening result
   ○ No evidence of alcohol-related problems
   ○ Potential alcohol problem (positive response to either question 15.a. or 15.b. and/or AUDIT-C (questions 15.c.-e.) score of 4 or more for men or 3 or more for women).
   Refer to PCM for evaluation.   ○ Yes   ○ No

6. During this deployment have you sought, or do you now intend to seek, counseling or care for your mental health?   ○ Yes   ○ No

7. Traumatic Brain Injury (TBI) risk assessment
   ○ No evidence of risk based on responses to questions 9.a. - d.
   ○ Potential TBI with persistent symptoms, based on responses to question 9.d.
   Refer for additional evaluation.   ○ Yes   ○ No

8. Tuberculosis risk assessment, based on response to question 20.
   ○ Minimal risk
   ○ Increased risk
   Recommend tuberculosis skin testing in 60-90 days   ○ Yes   ○ No

9. Depleted Uranium (DU) risk assessment, based on responses to question 16 (DU, Yes) or question 18 (Yes).
   ○ No evidence of exposure to depleted uranium
   ○ Potential exposure to depleted uranium
   Refer to PCM for completion of DD Form 2872 and possible 24-hour urinalysis.   ○ Yes   ○ No

10. Do you have any other concerns about possible exposures or events during this deployment that you feel may affect your health?   ○ Yes   ○ No
    Please list your concerns: _____

11. Do you currently have any questions or concerns about your health?   ○ Yes   ○ No
    Please list your concerns: _____

DD FORM 2796, JAN 2008   Page 6 of 7 Pages

This form must be completed electronically. Handwritten forms will not be accepted.

POST-DEPLOYMENT HEALTH RE-ASSESSMENT (PDHRA)

PRIVACY ACT STATEMENT

AUTHORITY: 10 U.S.C. 136, 1074f, 3013, 5013, 8013 and E.O. 9397.

PRINCIPAL PURPOSE(S): To assess your state of health after deployment in support of military operations and to assist military healthcare providers in identifying and providing present and future medical care you may need. The information you provide may result in a referral for additional healthcare that may include medical, dental or behavioral healthcare or diverse community support services.

ROUTINE USE(S): In addition to those disclosures generally permitted under 5 U.S.C. 552a(b) of the Privacy Act, to other Federal and State agencies and civilian healthcare providers, as necessary, in order to provide necessary medical care and treatment.

DISCLOSURE: Voluntary. If not provided, healthcare WILL BE furnished, but comprehensive care may not be possible.

INSTRUCTIONS: Please read each question completely and carefully before entering your response or marking your selection. **YOU ARE ENCOURAGED TO ANSWER EACH QUESTION.** Withholding or providing inaccurate information may impair a healthcare provider's ability to identify health problems and refer you to appropriate sources for additional evaluation or treatment. If you do not understand a question, please ask for help. Please respond based on your **MOST RECENT DEPLOYMENT.**

DEMOGRAPHICS

Last Name

First Name

Middle Initial

Social Security Number

Date of Birth *(dd/mmm/yyyy)*

Today's Date *(dd/mmm/yyyy)*

Date arrived theater *(dd/mmm/yyyy)*

Date departed theater *(dd/mmm/yyyy)*

SAMPLE

Gender
- ○ Male
- ○ Female

Marital Status
- ○ Never Married
- ○ Married
- ○ Separated
- ○ Divorced
- ○ Widowed

Service Branch
- ○ Air Force
- ○ Army
- ○ Navy
- ○ Marine Corps
- ○ Coast Guard
- ○ Civilian Employee
- ○ Other

Status Prior to Deployment
- ○ Active Duty
- ○ Selected Reserves - Reserve - Unit
- ○ Selected Reserves - Reserve - AGR
- ○ Selected Reserves - Reserve - IMA
- ○ Selected Reserves - National Guard - Unit
- ○ Selected Reserves - National Guard - AGR
- ○ Ready Reserves - IRR
- ○ Ready Reserves - ING
- ○ Civilian Government Employee
- ○ Other

Pay Grade

○ E1	○ O1	○ W1
○ E2	○ O2	○ W2
○ E3	○ O3	○ W3
○ E4	○ O4	○ W4
○ E5	○ O5	○ W5
○ E6	○ O6	
○ E7	○ O7	○ Other
○ E8	○ O8	
○ E9	○ .O9	
	○ O10	

Location of Operation
To what areas were you mainly deployed *(land-based operations more than 30 days)?* Please mark all that apply, including the number of months spent at each location.
- ○ Country 1 _____ Months
- ○ Country 2 _____ Months
- ○ Country 3 _____ Months
- ○ Country 4 _____ Months
- ○ Country 5 _____ Months

Since return from deployment I have:
- ○ Maintained/returned to previous status
- ○ Transitioned to Selected Reserves
- ○ Transitioned to IRR
- ○ Transitioned to ING
- ○ Retired from Military Service
- ○ Separated from Military Service

Current Contact Information:
Phone: _____
Cell: _____
DSN: _____
Email: _____
Address: _____
_____
_____

Total Deployments in Past 5 Years:

OIF	OEF	Other
○ 1	○ 1	○ 1
○ 2	○ 2	○ 2
○ 3	○ 3	○ 3
○ 4	○ 4	○ 4
○ 5 or more	○ 5 or more	○ 5 or more

Current Unit of Assignment
_____

Current Assignment Location
_____

Point of Contact who can always reach you:
Name: _____
Phone: _____
Email: _____
Mailing Address: _____

DD FORM 2900, JAN 2008   PREVIOUS EDITION IS OBSOLETE.

Page 1 of 5 Pages
Adobe Professional 7.0

This form must be completed electronically. Handwritten forms will not be accepted.

Service Member's Social Security Number:

1. Overall, how would you rate your health during the **PAST MONTH?**
   - ○ Excellent
   - ○ Very Good
   - ○ Good
   - ○ Fair
   - ○ Poor

2. Compared to before your most recent deployment, how would you rate your health in general now?
   - ○ Much better now than before I deployed
   - ○ Somewhat better now than before I deployed
   - ○ About the same as before I deployed
   - ○ Somewhat worse now than before I deployed
   - ○ Much worse now than before I deployed

3. During the past 4 weeks, how difficult have physical health problems *(illness or injury)* made it for you to do your work or other regular daily activities?
   - ○ Not difficult at all   ○ Very difficult
   - ○ Somewhat difficult   ○ Extremely difficult

4. During the past 4 weeks, how difficult have emotional problems *(such as feeling depressed or anxious)* made it for you to do your work, take care of things at home, or get along with other people?
   - ○ Not difficult at all   ○ Very difficult
   - ○ Somewhat difficult   ○ Extremely difficult

5. Since you returned from deployment, about how many times have you seen a healthcare provider for any reason, such as in sick call, emergency room, primary care, family doctor, or mental health provider?
   - ○ No visits   ○ 1 visit   ○ 2-3 visits   ○ 4-5 visits   ○ 6 or more

6. Since you returned from deployment, have you been hospitalized?   ○ Yes   ○ No

7. During your deployment, were you wounded, injured, assaulted or otherwise physically hurt?   ○ Yes   ○ No
   If **NO**, skip to Question 8.

7a. If **YES**, are you still having problems related to this wound, assault, or injury?   ○ Yes   ○ No   ○ Unsure

8. In addition to wounds or injuries you listed in question 7., do you currently have a health concern or condition that you feel is related to your deployment?   ○ Yes   ○ No   ○ Unsure
   If **NO**, skip to Question 9.

8a. If **YES**, please mark the item(s) that best describe your deployment-related condition or concern:

○ Fever		○ Dimming of vision, like the lights were going out	
○ Cough lasting more than 3 weeks		○ Chest pain or pressure	
○ Trouble breathing		○ Dizzy, light headed, passed out	
○ Bad headaches		○ Diarrhea, vomiting, or frequent indigestion/heartburn	
○ Generally feeling weak		○ Problems sleeping or still feeling tired after sleeping	
○ Muscle aches		○ Trouble concentrating, easily distracted	
○ Swollen, stiff or painful joints		○ Forgetful or trouble remembering things	
○ Back pain		○ Hard to make up your mind or make decisions	
○ Numbness or tingling in hands or feet		○ Increased irritability	
○ Trouble hearing		○ Taking more risks such as driving faster	
○ Ringing in the ears		○ Skin diseases or rashes	
○ Watery, red eyes		○ Other *(please list)*:	

9a. During this deployment, did you experience any of the following events? *(Mark all that apply)*

	Yes	No
(1) Blast or explosion *(IED, RPG, land mine, grenade, etc.)*	○	○
(2) Vehicular accident/crash *(any vehicle, including aircraft)*	○	○
(3) Fragment wound or bullet wound above your shoulders	○	○
(4) Fall	○	○
(5) Other event *(for example, a sports injury to your head)*. Describe:	○	○

9b. Did any of the following happen to you, or were you told happened to you, IMMEDIATELY after any of the event(s) you just noted in question 9a.? *(Mark all that apply)*

	Yes	No
(1) Lost consciousness or got "knocked out"	○	○
(2) Felt dazed, confused, or "saw stars"	○	○
(3) Didn't remember the event	○	○
(4) Had a concussion	○	○
(5) Had a head injury	○	○

c. Did any of the following problems begin or get worse after the event(s) you noted in question 9a.? *(Mark all that apply)*

	Yes	No
(1) Memory problems or lapses	○	○
(2) Balance problems or dizziness	○	○
(3) Ringing in the ears	○	○
(4) Sensitivity to bright light	○	○
(5) Irritability	○	○
(6) Headaches	○	○
(7) Sleep problems	○	○

d. In the past week, have you had any of the symptoms you indicated in 9c.? *(Mark all that apply)*

	Yes	No
(1) Memory problems or lapses	○	○
(2) Balance problems or dizziness	○	○
(3) Ringing in the ears	○	○
(4) Sensitivity to bright light	○	○
(5) Irritability	○	○
(6) Headaches	○	○
(7) Sleep problems	○	○

SAMPLE

DD FORM 2900, JAN 2008   Page 2 of 5 Pages

This form must be completed electronically. Handwritten forms will not be accepted.

Service Member's Social Security Number: _____

10. Do you have any persistent major concerns regarding the health effects of something you believe you may have been exposed to or encountered while deployed? ○ Yes ○ No
If **NO**, skip to question 11.

10a. If **YES**, please mark the item(s) that best describe your concern:

○ Animal bites	○ Loud noises
○ Animal bodies *(dead)*	○ Paints
○ Chlorine gas	○ Pesticides
○ Depleted uranium *(If yes, explain)* _____	○ Radar/Microwaves
○ Excessive vibration	○ Sand/dust
○ Fog oils (smoke screen	○ Smoke from burning trash or feces
○ Garbage	○ Smoke from oil fire
○ Human blood, body fluids, body parts, or dead bodies	○ Solvents
○ Industrial pollution	○ Tent heater smoke
○ Insect bites	○ Vehicle or truck exhaust fumes
○ Ionizing radiation	○ Other exposures to toxic chemicals or materials, such as ammonia, nitric acid, etc.: *(If yes, explain)*
○ JP8 or other fuels	
○ Lasers	

11. Since return from your deployment, have you had serious conflicts with your spouse, family members, close friends, or at work that continue to cause you worry or concern? ○ Yes ○ No ○ Unsure

12. Have you ever had any experience that was so frightening, horrible, or upsetting that, IN THE PAST MONTH, you ....

   a. Have had nightmares about it or thought about it when you did not want to? ○ Yes ○ No

   b. Tried hard not to think about it or went out of your way to avoid situations that remind you of it? ○ Yes ○ No

   c. Were constantly on guard, watchful, or easily startled? ○ Yes ○ No

   d. Felt numb or detached from others, activities, or your surroundings? ○ Yes ○ No

13a. In the PAST MONTH, Did you use alcohol more than you meant to? ○ Yes ○ No

   b. In the PAST MONTH, have you felt that you wanted to or needed to cut down on your drinking? ○ Yes ○ No

   c. How often do you have a drink containing alcohol?
     ○ Never ○ Monthly or less ○ 2 to 4 times a month ○ 2 to 3 times a week ○ 4 or more times a week

   d. How many drinks containing alcohol do you have on a typical day when you are drinking?
     ○ 1 or 2 ○ 3 or 4 ○ 5 or 6 ○ 7 to 9 ○ 10 or more

   e. How often do you have six or more drinks on one occasion?
     ○ Never ○ Less than monthly ○ Monthly ○ Weekly ○ Daily

14. Over the PAST MONTH, have you been bothered by the following problems?	Not at all	Few or several days	More than half the days	Nearly every day
a. Little interest or pleasure in doing things	○	○	○	○
b. Feeling down, depressed, or hopeless	○	○	○	○

15. Would you like to schedule a visit with a healthcare provider to further discuss your health concern(s)? ○ Yes ○ No

16. Are you currently interested in receiving information or assistance for a stress, emotional or alcohol concern? ○ Yes ○ No

17. Are you currently interested in receiving assistance for a family or relationship concern? ○ Yes ○ No

18. Would you like to schedule a visit with a chaplain or a community support counselor? ○ Yes ○ No

DD FORM 2900, JAN 2008   Page 3 of 5 Pages

APPENDICES

This form must be completed electronically. Handwritten forms will not be accepted.

Service Member's Social Security Number: Date *(dd/mmm/yyyy)*:

Health Care Provider Only

Provider Review and Interview

1. **Review symptoms and deployment concerns identified on form:**
   - ○ Confirmed screening results as reported
   - ○ Screening results modified, amended, clarified during interview:

2. **Ask behavioral risk questions. Conduct risk assessment.**
   - a. Over the PAST MONTH, have you been bothered by thoughts that you would be better off dead or of hurting yourself in some way?   ○ Yes   ○ No
   -    **IF YES**, about how often have you been bothered by these thoughts?   ○ Very few days   ○ More than half of the time   ○ Nearly every day
   - b. Since return from your deployment, have you had thoughts or concerns that you might hurt or lose control with someone?   ○ Yes   ○ No   ○ Unsure

3. **If member reports positive or unsure response to 2a. or 2b., conduct risk assessment.**
   - a. Does member pose a current risk for harm to self or others?   ○ No, not a current risk   ○ Yes, poses a current risk   ○ Unsure
   - b. Outcome of assessment   ○ Immediate referral   ○ Routine follow-up referral   ○ Referral not indicated

4. **Alcohol screening result**
   - ○ No evidence of alcohol-related problems.
   - ○ Potential alcohol problem (positive response to either question 13a. or 13b. and/or AUDIT-C (questions 13c.-e.) score of 4 or more for men or 3 or more for women). Refer to PCM for evaluation.   ○ Yes   ○ No

5. **Traumatic Brain Injury (TBI) risk assessment**
   - ○ No evidence of risk based on responses to questions 9.a. - d.
   - ○ Potential TBI with persistent symptoms, based on responses to question 9d.
   - Refer for additional evaluation.   ○ Yes   ○ No

6. **Record additional questions or concerns identified by patient during interview:**

_____

_____

_____

_____

_____

_____

_____

_____

_____

_____

_____

_____

_____

_____

_____

DD FORM 2900, JAN 2008   Page 4 of 5 Pages

This form must be completed electronically. Handwritten forms will not be accepted.

Service Member's Social Security Number: _____   **Date** *(dd/mmm/yyyy)*: _____

Assessment and Referral: After my interview with the service member and review of this form, there is a need for further evaluation and follow-up as indicated below. (More than one may be noted for patients with multiple concerns.)

7. Identified Concerns	Minor Concern	Major Concern	Already Under Care Yes	Already Under Care No	8. Referral Information	Within 24 hours	Within 7 days	Within 30 days
					a. Primary Care, Family Practice	○	○	○
○ Physical Symptom(s)	○	○	○	○	b. Behavioral Health in Primary Care	○	○	○
○ Exposure Symptom(s)	○	○	○	○	c. Mental Health Specialty Care	○	○	○
○ Depression symptoms	○	○	○	○	d. Other specialty care:			
○ PTSD symptoms	○	○	○	○	Audiology	○	○	○
○ Anger/Aggression	○	○	○	○	Cardiology	○	○	○
○ Suicidal Ideation	○	○	○	○	Dentistry	○	○	○
○ Social/Family Conflict	○	○	○	○	Dermatology	○	○	○
○ Alcohol Use	○	○	○	○	ENT	○	○	○
○ Other: _____	○	○	○	○	GI	○	○	○
9. Comments:					Internal Medicine	○	○	○
_____					Neurology	○	○	○
_____					OB/GYN	○	○	○
_____					Ophthalmology	○	○	○
_____					Optometry	○	○	○
_____					Orthopedics	○	○	○
_____					Pulmonology	○	○	○
_____					Urology	○	○	○
_____					e. Case Manager, Care Manager	○	○	○
_____					f. Substance Abuse Program	○	○	○
_____					g. Health Promotion, Health Education	○	○	○
_____					h. Chaplain	○	○	○
_____					i. Family Support, Community Service	○	○	○
_____					j. Military OneSource	○	○	○
_____					k. Other: _____	○	○	○
_____					l. No referral made ○			

I certify that this review process has been completed.

10. Provider's signature and stamp:

ICD-9 Code for this visit: V70.5 _ F

Ancillary Staff/Administrative Section

11. Member was provided the following:	12. Referral was made to the following healthcare or support system:
○ Health Education and Information	○ Military Treatment Facility
○ Health Care Benefits and Resources Information	○ Division/Line-based medical resource
○ Appointment Assistance	○ VA Medical Center or Community Clinic
○ Service member declined to complete form	○ Vet Center
○ Service member declined to complete interview/assessment	○ TRICARE Provider
○ Service member declined referral for services	○ Contract Support: _____
○ LOD	○ Community Service: _____
○ Other: _____	○ Other: _____
	○ None

DD FORM 2900, JAN 2008   Page 5 of 5 Pages

MENTAL HEALTH NEEDS OF SOLDIERS INCREASE SEVERAL MONTHS AFTER RETURNING FROM IRAQ WAR

CHICAGO—Compared to initial screening upon returning from the Iraq war, U.S. soldiers report increased mental health concerns and needs several months after their return for problems such as post-traumatic stress disorder and depression, according to a study in the November 14 issue of *The Journal of the American Medical Association (JAMA)*.

"Our previous article described the Department of Defense's (DoD) screening efforts to identify mental health concerns among soldiers and Marines as they return from Iraq and Afghanistan using the Post-Deployment Health Assessment (PDHA). However, the article also raised concerns that mental health problems might be missed because of the early timing of this screening. It cited preliminary data showing that soldiers were more likely to indicate mental health distress several months after return than upon their immediate return. Based on these preliminary data, the DoD initiated a second screening similar to the first, to occur 3 to 6 months after return from deployment," the authors write.

Charles S. Milliken, M.D., of Walter Reed Army Institute of Research, U.S. Army Medical Research and Materiel Command, Silver Spring, Md., and colleagues analyzed the mental health responses of the first cohort of soldiers (n = 88,235) to complete both the initial screening and the new later screening, with a median (midpoint) of six months between the two assessments. Both screenings included a self-report questionnaire and a brief interview with a clinician.

The researchers found that soldiers reported more mental health concerns, such as post-traumatic stress disorder (PTSD), major depression or alcohol misuse during the later screening. Of the 88,235 soldiers, 3,925 (4.4 percent) were referred for mental health care during the initial screening and 10,288 (11.7 percent) were referred during the later screening. Combined data from both screenings showed that the clinicians identified 20.3 percent of active and 42.4 percent of reserve soldiers as needing referral or already being under care for mental health problems.

Among active component soldiers, use of mental health services increased substantially following the later screening, especially within 30 days of the assessment. The majority of all soldiers who accessed mental health care (74 percent, n = 9,074) had not been identified as needing referral.

Concerns about interpersonal conflict increased four-fold between the two screenings. Soldiers frequently reported alcohol concerns, yet very few were referred to alcohol treatment. Although soldiers were much more likely to report PTSD symptoms on the later screening instrument, 49 percent to 59 percent of those who had PTSD symptoms identified on the initial screen improved by the time they took the later screen, suggesting that the increase was due to new symptoms being reported.

"The study shows that the rates that we previously reported based on surveys taken immediately on return from deployment substantially underestimate the mental health burden," the authors write. "This emphasizes the enormous opportunity for a better-resourced DoD mental health system to intervene early before soldiers leave active duty.

"Increased relationship problems underscore shortcomings in services for family members. Reserve component soldiers who had returned to civilian status were referred at higher rates on the [later screening], which could reflect their concerns about their ongoing health coverage. Lack of confidentiality may deter soldiers with alcohol problems from accessing treatment. In the context of an overburdened system of care, the effectiveness of population mental health screening was difficult to ascertain."

Editor's Note: Please see the article for additional information, including other authors, author contributions and affiliations, financial disclosures, funding and support, etc.

An Achievable Vision:

Report of the
Department of Defense
Task Force on Mental Health
June 2007

EXECUTIVE SUMMARY

Background

Section 723 of the National Defense Authorization Act for fiscal year 2006 directed the Secretary of Defense to "establish within the Department of Defense a task force to examine matters relating to mental health and the Armed Forces" and produce "a report containing an assessment of, and recommendations for improving, the efficacy of mental health services provided to members of the Armed Forces by the Department of Defense." Towards that end, the Department of Defense Task Force on Mental Health (Task Force) was established, comprising seven military and seven civilian professionals with mental health expertise. Task Force members were appointed in May 2006, with one military and one civilian member serving as co-chairs for the group. Lieutenant General Kevin C. Kiley, the Surgeon General of the Army, served as the military co-chair from the inception of the Task Force to March 2007. Vice Admiral Donald C. Arthur, the Surgeon General of the Navy, served as the military co-chair from April 2007 to June 2007. Dr. Shelley MacDermid, director of the Military Family Research Institute at Purdue University, served as the elected civilian co-chair for the duration of the Task Force, from May 2006 to June 2007.

The Task Force acknowledges the good-faith efforts currently being implemented by the Department of Defense and the military Services. In the history of warfare, no other nation or its leadership has invested such an intensive or sophisticated effort across all echelons to support the psychological health of its military service members and families as the Department of Defense has invested during the Global War on Terrorism. These laudable efforts acknowledged, the actual success of the overall effort must be evaluated as a function of the effectiveness of resource allocation and the design, execution, and refinement of strategies.

Introduction

The costs of military service are substantial. Many costs are readily apparent; others are less apparent but no less important. Among the most pervasive and potentially disabling consequences of these costs is the threat to the psychological health of our nation's fighting forces, their families, and their survivors. Our involvement in the Global War on Terrorism has created unforeseen demands not only on individual military service members and their families, but also on the Department of Defense itself, which must expand its capabilities to support the psychological health of its service members and their families.

The system of care for psychological health that has evolved over recent decades is insufficient to meet the needs of today's forces and their beneficiaries, and will not be sufficient to meet their needs in the future.

In particular, the system is being challenged by emergence of two "signature injuries" from the current conflict – post-traumatic stress disorder and traumatic brain injury. These two injuries often coincide, requiring integrated and interdisciplinary treatment methods. New demands have exposed shortfalls in a health care system that in previous decades had been oriented away from a wartime focus. Staffing levels were poorly matched to the high operational tempo even prior to the current conflict, and the system has become even more strained by the increased deployment of active duty providers with mental health expertise. As such, the system of care for psychological health that has evolved over recent decades is insufficient to meet the needs of today's forces and their beneficiaries, and will not be sufficient to meet their needs in the future.

Changes in the military mental health system and military medicine more generally, have mirrored trends in the landscape of American healthcare toward acute, short-term treatment models that may not provide optimal management of psychological disorders that tend to be more chronic in nature. As in the civilian sector, military mental health practices tend to emphasize identification and treatment of specific disorders over preventing and treating illness, enhancing coping, and maximizing resilience. Emerging lessons from recent deployments have

APPENDICES

raised questions about the adequacy of this orientation, not only for treating psychological disorders, but also for achieving the goal of a healthy and resilient force.

The challenges are enormous and the consequences of non-performance are significant. Data from the Post-Deployment Health Re-Assessment, which is administered to service members 90 to 120 days after returning from deployment, indicate that 38 percent of Soldiers and 31 percent of Marines report psychological symptoms. Among members of the National Guard, the figure rises to 49 percent (U.S. Air Force, 2007; U.S. Army, 2007; U.S. Navy, 2007). Further, psychological concerns are significantly higher among those with repeated deployments, a rapidly growing cohort. Psychological concerns among family members of deployed and returning Operation Iraqi Freedom and Operation Enduring Freedom veterans, while yet to be fully quantified, are also an issue of concern. Hundreds of thousands of children have experienced the deployment of a parent.

Vision

Maintaining the psychological health, enhancing the resilience, and ensuring the recovery of service members and their families are essential to maintaining a ready and fully capable military force. Towards that end, the Task Force's vision for a transformed military system requires the fulfillment of four interconnected goals:

1) A culture of support for psychological health, wherein all service members and leaders will be educated to understand that psychological health is essential to overall health and performance, will be fostered. Early and non-stigmatizing psychological health assessments and referrals to services will be routine and expected.

2) Service members and their families will be psychologically prepared to carry out their missions. Service members and their families will receive a full continuum of excellent care in both peacetime and wartime, particularly when service members have been injured or wounded in the course of duty.

3) Sufficient and appropriate resources will be allocated to prevention, early intervention, and treatment in both the Direct Care and TRICARE Network systems, and will be distributed according to need.

4) At all levels, visible and empowered leaders will advocate, monitor, plan, coordinate and integrate prevention, early intervention, and treatment.

Together, these interconnected and interdependent objectives define an achievable future. Until each goal is fulfilled, service members and their families will be inadequately served.

Findings

In general, the Task Force found that current efforts fall significantly short of achieving each of the goals enumerated above. This assessment was based on a review of available research and survey data, additional data sought specifically by the Task Force, public testimony from experts and advocates, and site visits to 38 military installations throughout the world, including the largest deployment platforms, where thousands of service members, their family members, commanders, mental health professionals, and community partners were given the opportunity to provide their input.

The Task Force arrived at a single finding underpinning all others: The Military Health System lacks the fiscal resources and the fully-trained personnel to fulfill its mission to support psychological health in peacetime or fulfill the enhanced requirements imposed during times of conflict. The mission of caring for psychological health has fundamentally changed and the current system must be restructured to reflect these changes. This requires acknowledgement of new fiscal and personnel requirements necessary to meet current and future demands for a full spectrum of services including: resilience-building, assessment, prevention, early intervention, and provision of an

173

Recommendations

Actionable recommendations to address the shortfalls outlined above are presented and discussed in the body of this document. These recommendations are designed to address the needs of members of the Active and Reserve Components, their eligible beneficiaries, and other Department of Defense beneficiaries. The Task Force's recommendations are categorized and summarized briefly below:

1) *Building a culture of support for psychological health*

   - Dispel stigma
   - Make mental health professionals easily accessible
   - Embed psychological health training throughout military life
   - Revise military policies to reflect current knowledge about psychological health
   - Make psychological assessment procedures an effective, efficient, and normal part of military life

2) *Ensuring a full continuum of excellent care for service members and their families*

   - Make prevention, early intervention, and treatment universally available
   - Maintain continuity of care across transitions
   - Ensure high-quality care
   - Provide family members with access to excellent care

3) *Providing sufficient resources and allocating them according to requirements*

   - Provide adequate resources for mental health services
   - Allocate staff according to need
   - Ensure an adequate supply of military providers
   - Ensure TRICARE networks fulfill beneficiaries' mental health needs

4) *Empowering leadership*

   - Establish visible leadership and advocacy for psychological health
   - Formalize collaboration at the installation, Service and Department of Defense levels to coordinate care for the psychological health of military service members

Conclusion

Against the backdrop of the Global War on Terror, the psychological health needs of America's military service members, their families, and their survivors pose a daunting and growing challenge to the Department of Defense. Although it is acknowledged that the work of the Task Force is necessarily incomplete and that the recommendations presented herein provide only the groundwork for a comprehensive strategic plan to support the psychological health of service members and their families, the immediacy of these needs imparts a sense of urgency to this report. As such, the Task Force urges the Department of Defense to adopt a similar sense of urgency in rapidly developing and implementing a plan of action.

APPENDICES

easily-accessible continuum of treatment for psychological health of service members and their families in both the Active and Reserve Components.

The Task Force's findings related to each of the four goals related to the vision discussed above are summarized briefly below:

1) *Building a culture of support for psychological health*
   - Stigma in the military remains pervasive and often prevents service members from seeking needed care.
   - Mental health professionals are not sufficiently accessible to service members.
   - Leaders, family members, and medical personnel are insufficiently trained in matters relating to psychological health.
   - Some Department of Defense policies, including those related to command notification or self-disclosure of psychological health issues, are overly conservative.
   - Existing processes for psychological assessment are insufficient to overcome the stigma inherent in seeking mental health services.

2) *Ensuring a full continuum of excellent care for service members and their families*
   - Significant gaps in the continuum of care for psychological health remain, specifically related to which services are offered, where services are offered, and who receives services.
   - Continuity of care is often disrupted during transitions among providers.
   - There are not sufficient mechanisms in place to assure the use of evidence-based treatments or the monitoring of treatment effectiveness
   - Family members have difficulty obtaining adequate mental health treatment.

3) *Providing sufficient resources and allocating them according to requirements*
   - The military system does not have enough fiscal or personnel resources to adequately support the psychological health of service members and their families in peace and during conflict.
   - Military treatment facilities lack the resources to provide a full continuum of psychological health care services for active duty service members and their families.
   - The number of active duty mental health professionals is insufficient and likely to decrease without substantial intervention.
   - The TRICARE network benefit for psychological health is hindered by fragmented rules and policies, inadequate oversight, and insufficient reimbursement.

4) *Empowering leadership*
   - Provision of a continuum of support for psychological health for military members and their families depends on the cooperation of many organizations with different authority structures and funding streams.
   - The Task Force found insufficient collaboration among organizations at the installation, Service and Department of Defense levels to provide and coordinate care for the psychological health of service members and their families.

MENTAL HEALTH PROBLEMS AND COMBAT DUTY

Combat Duty in Iraq and Afghanistan, Mental Health Problems, and Barriers to Care

Charles W. Hoge, M.D., Carl A. Castro, Ph.D., Stephen C. Messer, Ph.D., Dennis McGurk, Ph.D., Dave I. Cotting, Ph.D., and Robert L. Koffman, M.D., M.P.H.

ABSTRACT

BACKGROUND

The current combat operations in Iraq and Afghanistan have involved U.S. military personnel in major ground combat and hazardous security duty. Studies are needed to systematically assess the mental health of members of the armed services who have participated in these operations and to inform policy with regard to the optimal delivery of mental health care to returning veterans.

METHODS

We studied members of four U.S. combat infantry units (three Army units and one Marine Corps unit) using an anonymous survey that was administered to the subjects either before their deployment to Iraq (n=2530) or three to four months after their return from combat duty in Iraq or Afghanistan (n=3671). The outcomes included major depression, generalized anxiety, and post-traumatic stress disorder (PTSD), which were evaluated on the basis of standardized, self-administered screening instruments.

RESULTS

Exposure to combat was significantly greater among those who were deployed to Iraq than among those deployed to Afghanistan. The percentage of study subjects whose responses met the screening criteria for major depression, generalized anxiety, or PTSD was significantly higher after duty in Iraq (15.6 to 17.1 percent) than after duty in Afghanistan (11.2 percent) or before deployment to Iraq (9.3 percent); the largest difference was in the rate of PTSD. Of those whose responses were positive for a mental disorder, only 23 to 40 percent sought mental health care. Those whose responses were positive for a mental disorder were twice as likely as those whose responses were negative to report concern about possible stigmatization and other barriers to seeking mental health care.

CONCLUSIONS

This study provides an initial look at the mental health of members of the Army and the Marine Corps who were involved in combat operations in Iraq and Afghanistan. Our findings indicate that among the study groups there was a significant risk of mental health problems and that the subjects reported important barriers to receiving mental health services, particularly the perception of stigma among those most in need of such care.

From the Department of Psychiatry and Behavioral Sciences, Walter Reed Army Institute of Research, U.S. Army Medical Research and Materiel Command, Silver Spring, Md. (C.W.H., C.A.C., S.C.M., D.M., D.I.C.); and First Naval Construction Division, Norfolk, Va. (R.L.K.). Address reprint requests to Dr. Hoge at the Department of Psychiatry and Behavioral Sciences, Walter Reed Army Institute of Research, 503 Robert Grant Ave., Silver Spring, MD 20910, or at charles.hoge@na.amedd.army.mil.

N Engl J Med 2004;351:13-22.
Copyright © 2004 Massachusetts Medical Society.

The NEW ENGLAND JOURNAL *of* MEDICINE

THE RECENT MILITARY OPERATIONS IN Iraq and Afghanistan, which have involved the first sustained ground combat undertaken by the United States since the war in Vietnam, raise important questions about the effect of the experience on the mental health of members of the military services who have been deployed there. Research conducted after other military conflicts has shown that deployment stressors and exposure to combat result in considerable risks of mental health problems, including post-traumatic stress disorder (PTSD), major depression, substance abuse, impairment in social functioning and in the ability to work, and the increased use of health care services.[1-8] One study that was conducted just before the military operations in Iraq and Afghanistan began found that at least 6 percent of all U.S. military service members on active duty receive treatment for a mental disorder each year.[9] Given the ongoing military operations in Iraq and Afghanistan, mental disorders are likely to remain an important health care concern among those serving there.

Many gaps exist in the understanding of the full psychosocial effect of combat. The all-volunteer force deployed to Iraq and Afghanistan and the type of warfare conducted in these regions are very different from those involved in past wars, differences that highlight the need for studies of members of the armed services who are involved in the current operations. Most studies that have examined the effects of combat on mental health were conducted among veterans years after their military service had ended.[1-8] A problem in the methods of such studies is the long recall period after exposure to combat.[10] Very few studies have examined a broad range of mental health outcomes near to the time of subjects' deployment.

Little of the existing research is useful in guiding policy with regard to how best to promote access to and the delivery of mental health care to members of the armed services. Although screening for mental health problems is now routine both before and after deployment[11] and is encouraged in primary care settings,[12] we are not aware of any studies that have assessed the use of mental health care, the perceived need for such care, and the perceived barriers to treatment among members of the military services before or after combat deployment.

We studied the prevalence of mental health problems among members of the U.S. armed services who were recruited from comparable combat units before or after their deployment to Iraq or Afghanistan. We identified the proportion of service members with mental health concerns who were not receiving care and the barriers they perceived to accessing and receiving such care.

METHODS

STUDY GROUPS

We summarized data from the first, cross-sectional phase of a longitudinal study of the effect of combat on the mental health of the soldiers and Marines deployed in Operation Iraqi Freedom and in Operation Enduring Freedom in Afghanistan. Three comparable U.S. Army units were studied with the use of an anonymous survey administered either before deployment to Iraq or after their return from Iraq or Afghanistan. Although no data from before deployment were available for the Marines in the study, data were collected from a Marine Corps unit after its return from Iraq that provided a basis for comparison with data obtained from Army soldiers after their return from Iraq.

The study groups included 2530 soldiers from an Army infantry brigade of the 82nd Airborne Division, whose responses to the survey were obtained in January 2003, one week before a year-long deployment to Iraq; 1962 soldiers from an Army infantry brigade of the 82nd Airborne Division, whose responses were obtained in March 2003, after the soldiers' return from a six-month deployment to Afghanistan; 894 soldiers from an Army infantry brigade of the 3rd Infantry Division, whose responses were obtained in December 2003, after their return from an eight-month deployment to Iraq; and 815 Marines from two battalions under the command of the 1st Marine Expeditionary Force, whose responses were obtained in October or November 2003, after a six-month deployment to Iraq. The 3rd Infantry Division and the Marine battalions had spearheaded early ground-combat operations in Iraq, in March through May 2003. All the units whose members responded to the survey were also involved in hazardous security duties. The questionnaires administered to soldiers and Marines after deployment to Iraq or Afghanistan were administered three to four months after their return to the United States. This interval allowed time in which the soldiers completed leave, made the transition back to garrison work duties, and had the opportunity to seek medical or mental health treatment, if needed.

RECRUITMENT AND REPRESENTATIVENESS OF THE SAMPLE

Unit leaders assembled the soldiers and Marines near their workplaces at convenient times, and the study investigators then gave a short recruitment briefing and obtained written informed consent on forms that included statements about the purpose of the survey, the voluntary nature of participation, and the methods used to ensure participants' anonymity. Overall, 58 percent of the soldiers and Marines from the selected units were available to attend the recruitment briefings (79 percent of the soldiers before deployment, 58 percent of the soldiers after deployment in Operation Enduring Freedom in Afghanistan, 34 percent of the soldiers after deployment in Operation Iraqi Freedom, and 65 percent of the Marines after deployment in Operation Iraqi Freedom). Most of those who did not attend the briefings were not available because of their rigorous work and training schedules (e.g., night training and post security).

A response was defined as completion of any part of the survey. The response rate among the soldiers and Marines who were briefed was 98 percent for the four samples combined. The rates of missing values for individual items in the survey were generally less than 15 percent; 2 percent of participants did not complete the PTSD measures, 5 percent did not complete the depression and anxiety measures, and 7 to 8 percent did not complete the items related to the use of alcohol. The high response rate was probably owing to the anonymous nature of the survey and to the fact that participants were given time by their units to complete the 45-minute survey. The study was conducted under a protocol approved by the institutional review board of the Walter Reed Army Institute of Research.

To assess whether or not our sample was representative, we compared the demographic characteristics of respondents with those of all active-duty Army and Marine personnel deployed to Operation Iraqi Freedom and Operation Enduring Freedom, using the Defense Medical Surveillance System.[13]

SURVEY AND MENTAL HEALTH OUTCOMES

The study outcomes were focused on current symptoms (i.e., those occurring in the past month) of a major depressive disorder, a generalized anxiety disorder, and PTSD. We used two case definitions for each disorder, a broad screening definition that followed current psychiatric diagnostic criteria[14] but did not include criteria for functional impairment or for severity, and a strict (conservative) screening definition that required a self-report of substantial functional impairment or a large number of symptoms. Major depression and generalized anxiety were measured with the use of the patient health questionnaire developed by Spitzer et al.[15-17] For the strict definition to be met, there also had to be evidence of impairment in work, at home, or in interpersonal functioning that was categorized as at the "very difficult" level as measured by the patient health questionnaire. The generalized anxiety measure was modified slightly to avoid redundancy; items that pertained to concentration, fatigue, and sleep disturbance were drawn from the depression measure.

The presence or absence of PTSD was evaluated with the use of the 17-item National Center for PTSD Checklist of the Department of Veterans Affairs.[4,8,18,19] Symptoms were related to any stressful experience (in the wording of the "specific stressor" version of the checklist), so that the outcome would be independent of predictors (i.e., before or after deployment). Results were scored as positive if subjects reported at least one intrusion symptom, three avoidance symptoms, and two hyperarousal symptoms[14] that were categorized as at the moderate level, according to the PTSD checklist. For the strict definition to be met, the total score also had to be at least 50 on a scale of 17 to 85 (with a higher number indicating a greater number of symptoms or greater severity), which is a well-established cutoff.[4,8,18,19] Misuse of alcohol was measured with the use of a two-question screening instrument.[20]

In addition to these measures, on the survey participants were asked whether they were currently experiencing stress, emotional problems, problems related to the use of alcohol, or family problems and, if so, whether the level of these problems was mild, moderate, or severe; the participants were then asked whether they were interested in receiving help for these problems. Subjects were also asked about their use of professional mental health services in the past month or the past year and about perceived barriers to mental health treatment, particularly stigmatization as a result of receiving such treatment.[21] Combat experiences were modified from previous scales.[22]

QUALITY-CONTROL PROCEDURES AND ANALYSIS

Responses to the survey were scanned with the use of ScanTools software (Pearson NCS). Quality-

The NEW ENGLAND JOURNAL *of* MEDICINE

control procedures identified scanning errors in no more than 0.38 percent of the fields (range, 0.01 to 0.38 percent). SPSS software (version 12.0) was used to conduct the analyses, including multiple logistic regression that was used to control for differences in demographic characteristics of members of study groups before and after deployment.[23,24]

RESULTS

The demographic characteristics of participants from the three Army units were similar. The Marines in the study were somewhat younger than the soldiers in the study and less likely to be married. The demographic characteristics of all the participants in the survey samples were very similar to those of the general, deployed, active-duty infantry population, except that officers were undersampled, which resulted in slightly lower age and rank distributions (Table 1). Data for the reference populations were obtained from the Defense Medical Surveillance System with the use of available rosters of Army and Marine personnel deployed to Iraq or Afghanistan in 2003 (Table 1).

Among the 1709 soldiers and Marines who had returned from Iraq the reported rates of combat experiences and frequency of contact with the enemy were much higher than those reported by soldiers who had returned from Afghanistan (Table 2). Only 31 percent of soldiers deployed to Afghanistan reported having engaged in a firefight, as compared with 71 to 86 percent of soldiers and Marines who had been deployed to Iraq. Among those who had been in a firefight, the median number of firefights during deployment was 2 (interquartile range, 1 to 3) among those in Afghanistan, as compared with 5 (interquartile range, 2 to 13; P<0.001 by analysis of variance) among soldiers deployed to Iraq and 5 (interquartile range, 3 to 10; P<0.001 by analysis of variance) among Marines deployed to Iraq.

Soldiers and Marines who had returned from Iraq were significantly more likely to report that they were currently experiencing a mental health problem, to express interest in receiving help, and to use mental health services than were soldiers returning from Afghanistan or those surveyed before deployment (Table 3). Rates of PTSD were significantly higher after combat duty in Iraq than before deployment, with similar odds ratios for the Army and Marine samples (Table 3). Significant associations were observed for major depression and the misuse of alcohol. Most of these associations re-

mained significant after control for demographic factors with the use of multiple logistic regression (Table 3). When the prevalence rates for any mental disorder were adjusted to match the distribution of officers and enlisted personnel in the reference populations, the result was less than a 10 percent decrease (range, 3.5 to 9.4 percent) in the rates shown in Table 3 according to both the broad and the strict definitions (data not shown).

For all groups responding after deployment, there was a strong reported relation between combat experiences, such as being shot at, handling dead bodies, knowing someone who was killed, or killing enemy combatants, and the prevalence of PTSD. For example, among soldiers and Marines who had been deployed to Iraq, the prevalence of PTSD (according to the strict definition) increased in a linear manner with the number of firefights during deployment: 4.5 percent for no firefights, 9.3 percent for one to two firefights, 12.7 percent for three to five firefights, and 19.3 percent for more than five firefights (chi-square for linear trend, 49.44; P<0.001). Rates for those who had been deployed to Afghanistan were 4.5 percent, 8.2 percent, 8.3 percent, and 18.9 percent, respectively (chi-square for linear trend, 31.35; P<0.001). The percentage of participants who had been deployed to Iraq who reported being wounded or injured was 11.6 percent as compared with 4.6 percent for those who had been deployed to Afghanistan. The rates of PTSD were significantly associated with having been wounded or injured (odds ratio for those deployed to Iraq, 3.27; 95 percent confidence interval, 2.28 to 4.67; odds ratio for those deployed to Afghanistan, 2.49; 95 percent confidence interval, 1.35 to 4.40).

Of those whose responses met the screening criteria for a mental disorder according to the strict case definition, only 38 to 45 percent indicated an interest in receiving help, and only 23 to 40 percent reported having received professional help in the past year (Table 4). Those whose responses met these screening criteria were generally about two times as likely as those whose responses did not to report concern about being stigmatized and about other barriers to accessing and receiving mental health services (Table 5).

DISCUSSION

We investigated mental health outcomes among soldiers and Marines who had taken part in the ground-combat operations in Iraq and Afghani-

MENTAL HEALTH PROBLEMS AND COMBAT DUTY

Table 1. Demographic Characteristics of Study Groups of Soldiers and Marines as Compared with Reference Groups.*

Characteristic	Army Study Groups				Marine Study Group	Army Reference Group (N=61,742)	Marine Reference Group (N=20,194)
	Before Deployment to Iraq (N=2530)	After Deployment to Afghanistan (N=1962)	After Deployment to Iraq (N=894)	After Deployment to Iraq (N=815)			
			number (percent)				
Age							
18–24 yr	1647 (66)	1226 (63)	528 (59)	652 (80)		32,840 (53)	13,824 (69)
25–29 yr	496 (20)	387 (20)	206 (23)	114 (14)		13,737 (22)	3,174 (16)
30–39 yr	336 (13)	316 (16)	147 (16)	41 (5)		12,960 (21)	2,703 (13)
40 yr or older	34 (1)	28 (1)	13 (2)	4 (1)		2,205 (4)	493 (2)
Sex							
Male	2489 (99)	1934 (99)	879 (98)	815 (100)		61,201 (99)	20,090 (99.5)
Female	26 (1)	23 (1)	14 (2)			541 (1)	104 (0.5)
Race or ethnic group							
White	1749 (70)	1339 (69)	531 (60)	544 (68)		44,365 (72)	15,344 (76)
Black	208 (8)	198 (10)	185 (21)	53 (7)		7,904 (13)	1,213 (6)
Hispanic	331 (13)	254 (13)	102 (12)	141 (18)		6,140 (10)	2,642 (13)
Other	195 (8)	141 (7)	67 (8)	63 (8)		3,262 (5)	867 (4)
Education							
High-school graduate or less	1955 (78)	1514 (78)	726 (82)	728 (89)		48,561 (79)	16,892 (84)
Some college or other	202 (8)	153 (8)	73 (8)	29 (4)		3,260 (5)	346 (2)
College graduate	339 (14)	277 (14)	85 (10)	54 (7)		8,838 (14)	2,945 (15)
Military grade							
Enlisted personnel†							
E1–E4	1585 (63)	1170 (60)	613 (69)	601 (84)		33,823 (55)	13,744 (68)
E5–E6	614 (24)	524 (27)	228 (26)	77 (11)		14,813 (24)	2,850 (14)
E7–E9	116 (5)	91 (5)	23 (3)	8 (1)		3,819 (6)	607 (3)
Officer	200 (8)	168 (8)	30 (3)	26 (4)		9,287 (15)	2,993 (15)
Marital status							
Single	1142 (50)	908 (52)	355 (46)	455 (63)		32,636 (53)	12,332 (61)
Married	936 (41)	685 (39)	338 (43)	204 (28)		27,582 (45)	7,499 (37)
Other	199 (9)	168 (9)	85 (11)	65 (9)		1,485 (2)	363 (2)

* Data exclude missing values, because not all respondents answered every question. Percentages may not sum to 100 because of rounding. Data for the reference groups were obtained from the Defense Medical Surveillance System's deployment rosters of Army and Marine personnel deployed in Operation Iraqi Freedom and in Afghanistan in 2003. The total number of persons on these rosters was 315,999, of whom 229,034 (72 percent) were active-component personnel; the remaining 86,965 were members of the Reserve and National Guard; 97,906 (31 percent) had a designation of a combat-arms occupation. Of the 229,034 active-component service members, 81,936 (36 percent) had combat-arms occupations, including 61,742 soldiers and 20,194 Marines in the reference groups.
† Higher numbers indicate higher grades.

stan. Respondents to our survey who had been deployed to Iraq reported a very high level of combat experiences, with more than 90 percent of them reporting being shot at and a high percentage reporting handling dead bodies, knowing someone who was injured or killed, or killing an enemy combatant (Table 2). Close calls, such as having been saved from being wounded by wearing body armor, were not infrequent. Soldiers who served in Afghanistan reported lower but still substantial rates of such experiences in combat.

The percentage of study subjects whose responses met the screening criteria for major depression,

PTSD, or alcohol misuse was significantly higher among soldiers after deployment than before deployment, particularly with regard to PTSD. The linear relationship between the prevalence of PTSD and the number of firefights in which a soldier had been engaged was remarkably similar among soldiers returning from Iraq and Afghanistan, suggesting that differences in the prevalence according to location were largely a function of the greater frequency and intensity of combat in Iraq. The association between injury and the prevalence of PTSD supports the results of previous studies.[25]

These findings can be generalized to ground-

180

The NEW ENGLAND JOURNAL of MEDICINE

Table 2. Combat Experiences Reported by Members of the U.S. Army and Marine Corps after Deployment to Iraq or Afghanistan.*			
Experience	Army Groups		Marine Group
	Afghanistan (N=1962)	Iraq (N=894)	Iraq (N=815)
	number/total number (percent)		
Being attacked or ambushed	1139/1961 (58)	789/883 (89)	764/805 (95)
Receiving incoming artillery, rocket, or mortar fire	1648/1960 (84)	753/872 (86)	740/802 (92)
Being shot at or receiving small-arms fire	1302/1962 (66)	826/886 (93)	779/805 (97)
Shooting or directing fire at the enemy	534/1961 (27)	672/879 (77)	692/800 (87)
Being responsible for the death of an enemy combatant	229/1961 (12)	414/871 (48)	511/789 (65)
Being responsible for the death of a noncombatant	17/1961 (1)	116/861 (14)	219/794 (28)
Seeing dead bodies or human remains	771/1958 (39)	832/879 (95)	759/805 (94)
Handling or uncovering human remains	229/1961 (12)	443/881 (50)	455/800 (57)
Seeing dead or seriously injured Americans	591/1961 (30)	572/882 (65)	604/803 (75)
Knowing someone seriously injured or killed	850/1962 (43)	751/878 (86)	693/797 (87)
Participating in demining operations	314/1962 (16)	329/867 (38)	270/787 (34)
Seeing ill or injured women or children whom you were unable to help	907/1961 (46)	604/878 (69)	665/805 (83)
Being wounded or injured	90/1961 (5)	119/870 (14)	75/803 (9)
Had a close call, was shot or hit, but protective gear saved you	—†	67/879 (8)	77/805 (10)
Had a buddy shot or hit who was near you	—†	192/880 (22)	208/797 (26)
Clearing or searching homes or buildings	1108/1961 (57)	705/884 (80)	695/805 (86)
Engaging in hand-to-hand combat	51/1961 (3)	189/876 (22)	75/800 (9)
Saved the life of a soldier or civilian	125/1961 (6)	183/859 (21)	150/789 (19)

* Data exclude missing values, because not all respondents answered every question. Combat experiences are worded as in the survey.
† The question was not included in this survey.

combat units, which are estimated to represent about a quarter of all Army and Marine personnel participating in Operation Iraqi Freedom and Operation Enduring Freedom in Afghanistan (when members of the Reserve and the National Guard are included) and nearly 40 percent of all active-duty personnel (when Reservists and members of the National Guard are not included). The demographic characteristics of the subjects in our samples closely mirrored the demographic characteristics of this population. The somewhat lower proportion of officers had a minimal effect on the prevalence rates, and potential differences in demographic factors among the four study groups were controlled for in our analysis with the use of logistic regression.

One demonstration of the internal validity of our findings was the observation of similar prevalence rates for combat experiences and mental health outcomes among the subjects in the Army and the Marine Corps who had returned from deployment to Iraq, despite the different demographic characteristics of members of these units and their different levels of availability for recruitment into the study.

The cross-sectional design involving different units that was used in our study is not as strong as a longitudinal design. However, the comparability of the Army samples and the similarity in outcomes among subjects in the Army and Marine units surveyed after deployment to Iraq should generate confidence in the cross-sectional approach. Another limitation of our study is the potential selection bias resulting from the enrollment procedures, which were influenced by the practical realities that resulted from working with operational units. Although work schedules affected the availability of soldiers to take part in the survey, the effect is not likely to have biased our results. However, the selection procedures did not permit the enrollment of persons who had been severely wounded or those who may have been removed from the units for oth-

Table 3. Perceived Mental Health Problems and Percentage of Subjects Who Met the Screening Criteria for Major Depression, Generalized Anxiety, Post-Traumatic Stress Disorder, and Alcohol Misuse.*

Mental Health Problem	Army Study Groups					Marine Study Group	
	Before Deployment to Iraq (N=2530)	After Deployment to Afghanistan (N=1962)		After Deployment to Iraq (N=894)		After Deployment to Iraq (N=815)	
	no./total no. (%)	no./total no. (%)	OR (95% CI)	no./total no. (%)	OR (95% CI)	no./total no. (%)	OR (95% CI)
Perceived moderate or severe problem	323/2261 (14.3)	303/1769 (17.1)†‡		153/784 (19.5)†‡		123/720 (17.1)	
Currently interested in receiving professional help	211/2243 (9.4)	180/1769 (10.2)		131/786 (16.7)†‡		106/706 (15.0)†‡	
Received professional help in the past month§	108/2280 (4.7)	118/1780 (6.6)†‡		91/796 (11.4)†‡		70/742 (9.4)†‡	
Definition of mental disorder							
Broad definition							
Depression according to PHQ	275/2418 (11.4)	267/1885 (14.2)	1.29 (1.07–1.54)‡‡	128/840 (15.2)	1.40 (1.12–1.76)†‡	114/775 (14.7)	1.34 (1.06–1.70)¶
Anxiety according to PHQ	375/2419 (15.5)	324/1886 (17.2)	1.13 (0.96–1.33)	147/839 (17.5)	1.16 (0.94–1.43)	122/776 (15.7)	1.02 (0.81–1.27)
PTSD according to PCL	226/2414 (9.4)	224/1956 (11.5)	1.25 (1.03–1.52)¶	159/881 (18.0)	2.13 (1.71–2.66)†‡	161/811 (19.9)	2.40 (1.92–2.99)†‡
Any of above	522/2500 (20.9)	479/1958 (24.5)	1.23 (1.07–1.41)†‡	246/882 (27.9)	1.47 (1.23–1.75)†‡	237/813 (29.2)	1.56 (1.30–1.87)†
Strict definition							
Depression according to PHQ	128/2418 (5.3)	130/1885 (6.9)	1.33 (1.03–1.71)‡	66/840 (7.9)	1.53 (1.12–2.08)†‡	55/775 (7.1)	1.37 (0.99–1.90)
Anxiety according to PHQ	155/2419 (6.4)	140/1886 (7.4)	1.17 (0.92–1.48)	66/839 (7.9)	1.25 (0.92–1.68)	51/776 (6.6)	1.03 (0.74–1.43)
PTSD according to PCL	120/2414 (5.0)	121/1956 (6.2)	1.26 (0.97–1.64)	114/881 (12.9)	2.84 (2.17–3.72)†‡	99/811 (12.2)	2.66 (2.01–3.51)†‡
Any of above	233/2500 (9.3)	220/1958 (11.2)	1.23 (1.01–1.50)¶	151/882 (17.1)	2.01 (1.61–2.51)†‡	127/813 (15.6)	1.80 (1.43–2.27)†‡
Alcohol misuse							
Have you used alcohol more than you meant to?	405/2358 (17.2)	452/1844 (24.5)	1.57 (1.35–1.82)†‡	198/819 (24.2)	1.54 (1.27–1.86)†‡	268/756 (35.4)	2.65 (2.20–3.18)†‡
Have you felt you wanted or needed to cut down on your drinking?	289/2313 (12.5)	331/1821 (18.2)	1.56 (1.31–1.85)†‡	168/815 (20.6)	1.82 (1.47–2.24)†‡	219/744 (29.4)	2.92 (2.39–3.57)†‡

* Each study group who responded after deployment was compared with the group that responded before deployment, with the use of odds ratios (with 95 percent confidence intervals) and chi-square testing. Data exclude missing values, because not all respondents answered every question. OR denotes odds ratio, CI confidence interval, PHQ patient health questionnaire, PTSD post-traumatic stress disorder, and PCL the National Center for Post-Traumatic Stress Disorder Checklist.
† P<0.01 for the comparison of groups responding after deployment with the group responding before deployment, calculated with the use of the chi-square test.
‡ The result remained significant after multiple logistic regression was used to control for age, rank, educational level, marital status, and race or ethnic group.
§ Professional help was defined as help from a mental health professional, a general medical doctor, or a chaplain or other member of the clergy, in either a military or civilian treatment setting.
¶ P<0.05 for the comparison of groups responding after deployment with the group responding before deployment, calculated with the use of the chi-square test.

The NEW ENGLAND JOURNAL of MEDICINE

Table 4. Perceived Need for and Use of Mental Health Services among Soldiers and Marines Whose Survey Responses Met the Screening Criteria for Major Depression, Generalized Anxiety, or Post-Traumatic Stress Disorder.*

Outcome	Army Study Groups			Marine Study Group
	Before Deployment to Iraq (N=233)	After Deployment to Afghanistan (N=220)	After Deployment to Iraq (N=151)	After Deployment to Iraq (N=127)
	number/total number (percent)			
Need				
Acknowledged a problem	184/215 (86)	156/192 (81)	104/133 (78)	91/106 (86)
Interested in receiving help	85/212 (40)	75/196 (38)	58/134 (43)	47/105 (45)
Received professional help†				
In past year				
Overall (from any professional)	61/222 (28)	46/198 (23)	56/140 (40)	33/113 (29)
From a mental health professional	33/222 (15)	26/198 (13)	37/138 (27)	24/112 (21)
In past month				
Overall (from any professional)	39/218 (18)	34/196 (17)	44/136 (32)	23/112 (21)
From a mental health professional	24/218 (11)	25/196 (13)	29/136 (21)	16/111 (14)

* Data exclude missing values, because not all respondents answered every question.
† Professional help was defined as help from a mental health professional, a general medical doctor, or a chaplain or other member of the clergy, in either a military or civilian treatment setting.

er reasons, such as misconduct. Thus, our estimates of the prevalence of mental disorders are conservative, reflecting the prevalence among working, non-disabled combat personnel. The period immediately before a long combat deployment may not be the best time at which to measure baseline levels of distress. The magnitude of the differences between the responses before and after deployment is particularly striking, given the likelihood that the group responding before deployment was already experiencing levels of stress that were higher than normal.

The survey instruments used to screen for mental disorders in this study have been validated primarily in the settings of primary care and in clinical populations. The results therefore do not represent definitive diagnoses of persons in nonclinical populations such as our military samples. However, requiring evidence of functional impairment or a high number of symptoms, as we did, according to the strict case definitions, increases the specificity and positive predictive value of the survey measures.[26,27] This conservative approach suggested that as many as 9 percent of soldiers may be at risk for mental disorders before combat deployment, and as many as 11 to 17 percent may be at risk for such disorders three to four months after their return from combat deployment.

Although there are few published studies of the rates of PTSD among military personnel soon after their return from combat duty, studies of veterans conducted years after their service ended have shown a prevalence of current PTSD of 15 percent among Vietnam veterans[28] and 2 to 10 percent among veterans of the first Gulf War.[4,8] Rates of PTSD among the general adult population in the United States are 3 to 4 percent,[26] which are not dissimilar to the baseline rate of 5 percent observed in the sample of soldiers responding to the survey before deployment. Research has shown that the majority of persons in whom PTSD develops meet the criteria for the diagnosis of this disorder within the first three months after the traumatic event.[29] In our study, administering the surveys three to four months after the subjects had returned from deployment and at least six months after the heaviest combat operations was probably optimal for investigating the long-term risk of mental health problems associated with combat. We are continuing to examine this risk in repeated cross-sectional and longitudinal assessments involving the same units.

Our findings indicate that a small percentage of soldiers and Marines whose responses met the screening criteria for a mental disorder reported that they had received help from any mental health professional, a finding that parallels the results of civilian studies.[30-32] In the military, there are unique factors that contribute to resistance to seeking such help, particularly concern about how a soldier will be perceived by peers and by the leadership. Concern about stigma was disproportionately greatest among those most in need of help from mental health services. Soldiers and Marines whose responses were scored as positive for a mental disor-

MENTAL HEALTH PROBLEMS AND COMBAT DUTY

Table 5. Perceived Barriers to Seeking Mental Health Services among All Study Participants (Soldiers and Marines).*

Perceived Barrier	Respondents Who Met Screening Criteria for a Mental Disorder (N=731)	Respondents Who Did Not Meet Screening Criteria for a Mental Disorder (N=5422)
	no./total no. (%)	
I don't trust mental health professionals.	241/641 (38)	813/4820 (17)
I don't know where to get help.	143/639 (22)	303/4780 (6)
I don't have adequate transportation.	117/638 (18)	279/4770 (6)
It is difficult to schedule an appointment.	288/638 (45)	789/4748 (17)
There would be difficulty getting time off work for treatment.	354/643 (55)	1061/4743 (22)
Mental health care costs too much money.	159/638 (25)	456/4736 (10)
It would be too embarrassing.	260/641 (41)	852/4752 (18)
It would harm my career.	319/640 (50)	1134/4738 (24)
Members of my unit might have less confidence in me.	377/642 (59)	1472/4763 (31)
My unit leadership might treat me differently.	403/637 (63)	1562/4744 (33)
My leaders would blame me for the problem.	328/642 (51)	928/4769 (20)
I would be seen as weak.	413/640 (65)	1486/4732 (31)
Mental health care doesn't work.	158/638 (25)	444/4748 (9)

* Data exclude missing values, because not all respondents answered every question. Respondents were asked to rate "each of the possible concerns that might affect your decision to receive mental health counseling or services if you ever had a problem." Perceived barriers are worded as on the survey. The five possible responses ranged from "strongly disagree" to "strongly agree," with "agree" and "strongly agree" combined as a positive response.

der were twice as likely as those whose responses were scored as negative to show concern about being stigmatized and about other barriers to mental health care.

This finding has immediate public health implications. Efforts to address the problem of stigma and other barriers to seeking mental health care in the military should take into consideration outreach, education, and changes in the models of health care delivery, such as increases in the allocation of mental health services in primary care clinics and in the provision of confidential counseling by means of employee-assistance programs. Screening for major depression is becoming routine in military primary care settings,[12] but our study suggests that it should be expanded to include screening for PTSD. Many of these considerations are being addressed in new military programs.[33] Reducing the perception of stigma and the barriers to care among military personnel is a priority for research and a priority for the policymakers, clinicians, and leaders who are involved in providing care to those who have served in the armed forces.

Supported by the Military Operational Medicine Research Program, U.S. Army Medical Research and Materiel Command, Ft. Detrick, Md.

The views expressed in this article are those of the authors and do not reflect the official policy or position of the Department of the Army, the Department of Defense, the U.S. government, or any of the institutions with which the authors are affiliated.

We are indebted to the Walter Reed Army Institute of Research Land Combat Study Team: Lolita Burrell, Ph.D., Scott Killgore, Ph.D., Melba Stetz, Ph.D., Paul Bliese, Ph.D., Oscar Cabrera, Ph.D., Anthony Cox, M.S.W., Timothy Allison-Aipa, Ph.D., Karen Eaton, M.S., Graeme Bicknell, M.S.W., Alexander Vo, Ph.D., and Charles Milliken, M.D., for survey-instrument design and data collection; to Spencer Campbell, Ph.D., for coordination of data collection and scientific advice; to David Couch for supervising the data-collection teams, database management, scanning, and quality control; to Wanda Cook for design and production of surveys; to Allison Whitt for survey-production and data-collection support; to Lloyd Shanklin, Joshua Fejeran, Vilna Williams, and Crystal Ross for data-collection, quality-assurance, scanning, and field support; to Jennifer Auchterlonie for assistance with Defense Medical Surveillance System analyses; to Akeiya Briscoe-Cureton for travel and administrative support; to the leadership of the units that were studied and to our medical and mental health professional colleagues at Ft. Bragg, Ft. Stewart, Camp Lejeune, and Camp Pendleton; to the Walter Reed Army Institute of Research Office of Research Management; to David Orman, M.D., psychiatry consultant to the Army Surgeon General, Gregory Belenky, M.D., and Charles C. Engel, M.D., for advice and review of the study; and, most important, to the soldiers and Marines who participated in the study for their service.

APPENDICES

REFERENCES

1. The Centers for Disease Control Vietnam Experience Study Group. Health status of Vietnam veterans. I. Psychosocial characteristics. JAMA 1988;259:2701-7.
2. Helzer JE, Robins LN, McEvoy L. Posttraumatic stress disorder in the general population: findings of the Epidemiologic Catchment Area survey. N Engl J Med 1987; 317:1630-4.
3. Jordan BK, Schlenger WE, Hough R, et al. Lifetime and current prevalence of specific psychiatric disorders among Vietnam veterans and controls. Arch Gen Psychiatry 1991;48:207-15.
4. The Iowa Persian Gulf Study Group. Self-reported illness and health status among Gulf War veterans: a population-based study. JAMA 1997;277:238-45.
5. Kessler RC, Sonnega A, Bromet E, Hughes M, Nelson CB. Posttraumatic stress disorder in the National Comorbidity Survey. Arch Gen Psychiatry 1995;52:1048-60.
6. Prigerson HG, Maciejewski PK, Rosenheck RA. Population attributable fractions of psychiatric disorders and behavioral outcomes associated with combat exposures among US men. Am J Public Health 2002; 92:59-63.
7. *Idem.* Combat trauma: trauma with highest risk of delayed onset and unresolved posttraumatic stress disorder symptoms, unemployment, and abuse among men. J Nerv Ment Dis 2001;189:99-108.
8. Kang HK, Natelson BH, Mahan CM, Lee KY, Murphy FM. Post-traumatic stress disorder and chronic fatigue syndrome-like illness among Gulf War veterans: a population-based survey of 30,000 veterans. Am J Epidemiol 2003;157:141-8.
9. Hoge CW, Lesikar SE, Guevara R, et al. Mental disorders among U.S. military personnel in the 1990s: association with high levels of health care utilization and early military attrition. Am J Psychiatry 2002;159: 1576-83.
10. Wessely S, Unwin C, Hotopf M, et al. Stability of recall of military hazards over time: evidence from the Persian Gulf War of 1991. Br J Psychiatry 2003;183:314-22.
11. Wright KM, Huffman AH, Adler AB, Castro CA. Psychological screening program overview. Mil Med 2002;167:853-61.
12. VA/DoD clinical practice guideline for the management of major depressive disorder in adults. In: Major depressive disorder (MDD): clinical practice guidelines. Washington, D.C.: Veterans Health Administration, May 2000. (Publication no. 10Q-CPG/MDD-00.) (Accessed June 4, 2004, at http://www.oqp.med.va.gov/cpg/MDD/MDD_Base.htm.)
13. Rubertone MV, Brundage JF. The Defense Medical Surveillance System and the Department of Defense serum repository: glimpses of the future of public health surveillance. Am J Public Health 2002;92:1900-4.
14. Diagnostic and statistical manual of mental disorders. 4th ed. DSM-IV. Washington, D.C.: American Psychiatric Association, 1994.
15. Spitzer RL, Kroenke K, Williams JB. Validation and utility of a self-report version of PRIME-MD: the PHQ primary care study. JAMA 1999;282:1737-44.
16. Lowe B, Spitzer RL, Grafe K, et al. Comparative validity of three screening questionnaires for DSM-IV depressive disorders and physicians' diagnoses. J Affect Disord 2004; 8:131-40.
17. Henkel V, Mergl R, Kohnen R, Maier W, Moller HJ, Hegerl U. Identifying depression in primary care: a comparison of different methods in a prospective cohort study. BMJ 2003;326:200-1.
18. Blanchard EB, Jones-Alexander J, Buckley TC, Forneris CA. Psychometric properties of the PTSD Checklist (PCL). Behav Res Ther 1996;34:669-73.
19. Weathers FW, Litz BT, Herman DS, Huska JA, Keane TM. The PTSD checklist (PCL): reliability, validity, and diagnostic utility. San Antonio, Tex.: International Society of Traumatic Stress Studies, October 1993. abstract. (Accessed June 4, 2004, at http://www.pdhealth.mil/library/downloads/PCL_sychometrics.doc.)
20. Brown RL, Leonard T, Saunders LA, Papasouliotis O. A two-item conjoint screen for alcohol and other drug problems. J Am Board Fam Pract 2001;14:95-106.
21. Britt TW. The stigma of psychological problems in a work environment: evidence from the screening of service members returning from Bosnia. J Appl Soc Psychol 2000;30:1599-618.
22. Castro CA, Bienvenu RV, Hufmann AH, Adler AB. Soldier dimensions and operational readiness in U.S. Army forces deployed to Kosovo. Int Rev Armed Forces Med Serv 2000;73:191-200.
23. Kleinbaum DG, Kupper LL, Morgenstern H. Epidemiologic research: principles and quantitative methods. Belmont, Calif.: Lifetime Learning, 1982.
24. Menard S. Applied logistic regression analysis. 2nd ed. Thousand Oaks, Calif.: Sage, 2002.
25. Friedman MJ, Schnurr PP, McDonagh-Coyle A. Post-traumatic stress disorder in the military veteran. Psychiatr Clin North Am 1994;17:265-77.
26. Narrow WE, Rae DS, Robins LN, Regier DA. Revised prevalence estimates of mental disorders in the United States: using a clinical significance criterion to reconcile 2 surveys' estimates. Arch Gen Psychiatry 2002; 59:115-23.
27. Hoge CW, Messer SC, Castro CA. Pentagon employees after September 11, 2001. Psychiatr Serv 2004;55:319-20.
28. Schlenger WE, Kulka RA, Fairbank JA, et al. The prevalence of post-traumatic stress disorder in the Vietnam generation: a multimethod, multisource assessment of psychiatric disorder. J Trauma Stress 1992; 5:333-63.
29. Carlier IVE, Lamberts RD, Gersons BPR. Risk factors for posttraumatic stress symptomatology in police officers: a prospective analysis. J Nerv Ment Dis 1997;185: 498-506.
30. Kessler RC, Berglund P, Demler O, et al. The epidemiology of major depressive disorder: results from the National Comorbidity Survey Replication (NCS-R). JAMA 2003; 289:3095-105.
31. Regier DA, Narrow WE, Rae DS, Manderscheid RW, Locke BZ, Goodwin FK. The de facto US mental and addictive disorders service system: Epidemiologic Catchment Area prospective 1-year prevalence rates of disorders and services. Arch Gen Psychiatry 1993;50:85-94.
32. Kessler RC, McGonagle KA, Zhao S, et al. Lifetime and 12-month prevalence of DSM-III-R psychiatric disorders in the United States: results from the National Comorbidity Survey. Arch Gen Psychiatry 1994;51: 8-19.
33. Deployment Health Clinical Center. Deployment cycle support and clinicians — practice guidelines. (Accessed June 4, 2004, at http://www.pdhealth.mil.)
Copyright © 2004 Massachusetts Medical Society.

RESOURCES FOR VETERANS AND THEIR FAMILIES

National Center for Post-Traumatic Stress Disorder (NCPTSD)

The NCPTSD "aims to advance the clinical care and social welfare of U.S. veterans through research, education and training on PTSD and stress-related disorders." Website offers links and information on treatment for PTSD for soldiers and civilians, as well as several guides for personnel and their families. An excellent starting point for PTSD information.

National Center for PTSD
VA Medical Center (116D)
215 North Main St.
White River Junction, VT 05009
Ph. 802-296-6300
E-mail: ncptsd@va.gov
www.ncptsd.va.gov

National Institute of Mental Health—PTSD Booklet
A booklet for those who want to know more about PTSD, with a section dedicated to recognizing causes, stressors, and personal

symptoms. This is a governmental resource with a solid research base; not specifically tailored to veterans.

National Institute of Mental Health (NIMH)
Science Writing, Press, and Dissemination Branch
6001 Executive Blvd., Room 8184, MSC 9663
Bethesda, MD 20892-9663
Ph. 866-615-6464
E-mail: nimhinfo@nih.gov
www.nimh.nih.gov/health/publications/post-traumatic-stress-disorder-a-real-illness/summary.shtml

Department of Veterans Affairs – Readjustment Counseling Service (Vet Center)

The VA's Readjustment Counseling Service is available to any veteran—and his or her immediate family—who served in a combat zone and received a military campaign ribbon. The Vet Center's aim is to support and assist combat veterans in a range of services, including employment counseling and drug/alcohol assessments, as they transition from military to civilian life.

Department of Veterans Affairs
810 Vermont Ave., N.W.
Washington, DC 20420
Ph. 800-905-4675 (Eastern)
Ph. 866-496-8838 (Pacific)
E-mail: Steve.Reeves@va.gov
www.vetcenter.va.gov

Courage to Care Campaign

Courage to Care is a "new, electronic health campaign for military and civilian professionals serving the military community, as well as for military men, women and families. Courage to Care consists of electronic fact sheets on timely health topics relevant to military life that provide actionable information. Fact sheets range from "What Military Families Should Know about Depression," to "Helping Children Cope During Deployment." The content of these fact sheets is developed by leading military health experts. The campaign is sponsored by the Uniformed Services University of the Health Sciences (USUHS).

Uniformed Services University of the Health Sciences

4301 Jones Bridge Rd.

Bethesda, MD 20814

E-mail: courage_to_care@usuhs.mil

www.usuhs.mil/psy/courage.html

Military Veterans PTSD Reference Manual

This online reference manual offers a comprehensive look at the history of PTSD and its diagnosis over the last century. Works through causes, effects, traditional and non-traditional treatments. There is even a chapter on working with the Department of Veterans' Affairs, which outlines and offers tips for the claims and appeals processes.

www.ptsdmanual.com

Veterans and Families

Veterans and Families is a nonprofit organization run by—you guessed it—veterans and their families. This site provides a plethora of links and information, including the organization's own "Homecoming Preparedness Guide," which serves to educate both homecoming veterans and their families during what can be a stressful transition period.

Ph. 916-284-0778

www.veteransandfamilies.org

FURTHER READING

Armstrong, Keith, Suzanne Best, and Paul Domenici. *Courage After Fire: Coping Strategies for Troops Returning from Iraq and Afghanistan and Their Families*. Ulysses Press, 2005.

Grossman, Dave Christensen and Loren W. Christensen. *On Combat: The Psychology and Physiology of Deadly Conflict in War and in Peace*. PPCT Research Publications, 2007.

Hart, Ashley B., III. *An Operator's Manual for Combat PTSD: Essays for Coping*. Writer's Showcase Press, 2000.

Meagher, Ilona. *Moving a Nation to Care: Post-Traumatic Stress Disorder and America's Returning Troops*. Ig Publishing, 2007.

Roche, John D. *The Veteran's PTSD Handbook: How to File and Collect on Claims for Post-Traumatic Stress Disorder*. Potomac Books, 2007.

Tick, Edward. *War and the Soul: Healing Our Nation's Veterans from Post-Traumatic Stress Disorder*. Quest Books, 2005.

ENDNOTES

1. Humane Society letter to Secretary of Defense Donald Rumsfeld regarding the enforcement of General Order 1A (GO-1A). 2005. http://www/hsus.org/web-files/PDF/Letter_to_Rumsfeld-Soldiers_and_Dogs-3-29-05.pdf.

2. United States Marine Corps. *United States Marine Guidebook of Essential Subjects.* Washington DC: Marine Corps Institute, 1983.

3. Department of Defense Task Force on Mental Health. 2007. *An Achievable Vision: Report of the Department of Defense Task Force on Mental Health.* Falls Church, VA: Defense Health Board.

4. CBS News. "Suicide Epidemic Among Veterans." *CBSNews. com.* 13 November 2007.

5. Hoge, Charles W. "Longitudinal Assessment of Mental Health Problems Among Active and Reserve Component Soldiers Returning From the Iraq War," *The Journal of the American Medical Association,* 13 November 2007.

6. Zoroya, Gregg. "Soldiers' Divorce Rates Up Sharply." *USA Today,* 7 June 2005.

7. Sontag, Deborah. "Iraq Veteran's Descent; A Prosecutor's Choice." *The New York Times,* 20 January 2008.

8. Sontag, Deborah and Lizette Alvarez. "In More Cases, Combat Trauma Is Taking the Stand." *The New York Times,* 27 January 2008.

9. Springen, Karen. "Pets: Good for Your Health?" *Newsweek. com*, 11 January 2008.

10. Dormin, Rusty. "Iraq War Dog to Retire with Fallen Marine's Family." *CNN.com*, 21 December 2007.

11. Daddis, Gregory A. "Understanding Fear's Effect on Unit Effectiveness." *Military Review*, July–August 2004.

12. Sturkey, Marion F. *Warrior Culture of the U. S. Marines.* 2 ed. Plum Branch, SC: Heritage Press International, 2003.

13. Sontag, Deborah and Lizette Alvarez. "Across America, Deadly Echoes of Foreign Battles." *The New York Times*, 13 January 2008.

14. Rizzo, Albert A., Ken Graap, Robert N. Mclay, et al. "Virtual Iraq: Initial Case Reports from a VR Exposure Therapy Application for Combat-Related Post Traumatic Stress Disorder." *Office of Naval Research*, 15 July 2007.

15. Dennis Patrick Wood, Jennifer Murphy, Kristy Center, Robert McLay, Dennis Reeves, Jeff Pyne, Russell Shilling, and Brenda K. Wiederhold. *CyberPsychology & Behavior*, 1 April 2007, 10(2): 309-315. doi:10.1089/cpb.2006.9951.

16. Hoge, Charles W., Carl A. Castro, Stephen C. Messer, Dennis McGurk, Dave I. Cotting, and Robert L. Koffman. "Combat Duty in Iraq and Afghanistan,. Mental Health Problems, and Barriers to Care." *The New England Journal of Medicine*, 1 July 2004.

BIBLIOGRAPHY

ARTICLES

Alvarez, Lizette, and Deborah Sontag. "In More Cases, Combat Trauma Is Taking the Stand." *The New York Times*, 27 January 2008.

CBS News. "More Iraq Vets Seek Mental Health Care." 1 March 2006. http://www.cbsnews.com/stories/2006/03/01/iraq/main1357296.shtml?source=serch_story. Accessed 22 January 2008.

CBS News. "Suicide Epidemic Among Veterans." November 2007. http://www.cbsnews.com/stories/2007/11/13/cbsnews_investigates/main3496471shtml.

Daddis, Gregory A. "Understanding Fear's Effect on Unit Effectiveness." *Military Review*, July–August 2004. http://usacac.army.mil /cac/milreview/download/ English/JulAug04/ daddis.pdf.

Department of Defense Task Force on Mental Health. 2007. *An Achievable Vision: Report of the Department of Defense Task Force on Mental Health*. Falls Church, VA: Defense Health Board.

Dormin, Rusty. "Iraq War Dog to Retire with Fallen Marine's Family." 2007. *CNN.com*. http://www.cnn.com/2007/US/12/21/marine.dog/index.html. Accesssed 14 January 2008.

Elias, Marilyn. "Mental Disorders Are on the Rise among Afghanistan, Iraq Veterans." *USA Today*, 30 March 2005. http://www.usatoday.com/news/nation/2005-03-30 veterans-disorders_x.htm?loc=interstitialskip. Accessed 22 January 2008.

Fontana, Alan F., and Robert A. Rosenheck. "Recent Trends in VA Treatments of Post Traumatic Stress Disorder and Other Mental Disorders." *Health Affairs: The Policy Journal of the Health Sphere*. 2007. http://content.healthaffairs.org/cgi.comten.abstract.26.6/1720. Accessed 22 January 2008.

Hoge, Charles W., Carl A. Castro, Stephen C. Messer, Dennis McGurk, Dave I. Cotting, and Robert L. Koffman. "Combat Duty in Iraq and Afghanistan, Mental Health Problems, and Barriers to Care." *The New England Journal of Medicine*, 01 July 2004.

Hoge, Charles W., Jennifer L. Auchterlonie and Charles S. Milliken. "Mental Health Problems, Use of Mental Health Services, and Attrition from Military Services after Returning from Deployment to Iraq or Afghanistan." *The Journal of the American Medical Association,* 1 March 2006.

JAMA/Archives. "Mental Health Needs of Soldiers Increase Several Months After Returning From Iraq War." 13 November 2007. www.jamamedia.org.

Lorge, Elizabeth M. "Army Study Finds Delayed Combat Stress Reporting." *Army. Mil/News*, 14 November 2007. http://www.army.mil/news/2007/11/14/6090-army-study-finds-delayed-combat-stress-reporting/. Accessed 22 January 2008.

Mental Health Advisory Team, Operation Iraqi Freedom. "Review of Soldier Suicides" (Annex D), 16 December 2003. http://www.armymedicine.army. mil/news/mhat/mhat/Annex_D.pdf.

Milliken, Charles S., Jennifer L. Auchterlonie and Charles W. Hoge. "Longitude Assessment of Mental Health Problems Among Active and Reserve Compoent Soliders Returning From the Iraq War." *The Journal of the American Medical Association*, 14 November 2007.

Osterwell, Neil. "Iraq Vets Bringing Home Mental Health Needs as High Rate." *Medpage Today.* 2006. http://www.medpagetoday.com/Psychiatry? AnxietyStress/tb/2763 March 01. Accessed 22 January 2008.

Pacelle, Wayne. Letter to Secretary of Defense, Honorable Donald Rumsfeld, March 29, 2003. http://www.hsus.org/web-files/PDF/Letter_to_Rumsfeld-soldiers_and_Dogs-3-29-05.pdf.

Sontag, Deborah. "Across America, Deadly Echoes of Foreign Battles." *The New York Times*, 1 January 2008.

Sontag, Deborah. "An Iraq Veteran's Descent; a Prosecutor's Choice." *The New York Times*, 20 January 2008. http://www.nytimes.com/2008/01/20/ us/20vets.html?_r=1&scp=1&sq=Iraq+Veteran%27s+Descent%3B+a+Pros ecutor%27s+Choice+&st=nyt&oref=slogin. Accessed 22 January 2008.

Springen, Karen. "Pets: Good for Your Health?" *Newsweek.com*, 11 January 2008. http://www.newsweek.com/id/91445.

Suicide Risk Management and Surveillance Office. *Army Suicide Event Report (ASER)*, 2006.

Rizzo, Albert A., Ken Graap, Ropert N. Mclay, Karen Perlman, Barbara O. Rothbaum, Greg Reger, Thomas Parsons, JoAnn Defede and Jarrell Pair. "Virtual Iraq: Initial Case Reports from a VR Exposure Therapy Application for Combat-Related Post Traumatic Stress Disorder." *Office of Naval Research*, 15 July 2007.

Tyson, Ann Scott. "Repeat Iraq Tours Raise Risk of PTSD, Army Finds." *Washingtonpost.com*, 20 December 2006. http://www.washingtonpost. com/wp.dyn/content/article/2006/12/19/AR2006121901659.html.

Tyson, Ann Scott. "Troops' Mental Distress Tracked." *Washingtonpost.com*, 14 November 2007. www.washingtonpost.com. Accessed 22 January 2008.

BIBLIOGRAPHY

Vedamtam, Shankar. "Verterans Report Mental Distress" *Washingtonpost. com*, 1 March 2006. www.washingtonpost.com. Accessed 22 January 2008.

Wood, Dennis P., Jennifer A. Murphy, Kristy B.Center, Carol Russ, Robert N. Mclay, Dennis Reeves, Jeff Pyne, Russell Shilling, Jack Hagan and Brenda K. Wierhold. "Combat Related Post Traumatic Stress Disorder: A Multiple Case Report Using Virtual Reality Graded Exposure Therapy with Physiological Monitoring." *Office of Naval Research.* [database] Accessed 22 January 2008.

Zoroya, Gregg. "Soldiers' Divorce Rates Up Sharply." *USA Today*, 7 June 2005. http://www.usatoday.com/news/nation/2005-06-07-soldier-divorces_x.htm.

BOOKS

Crawford, John. *The Last True Story I'll Ever Tell.* New York: Riverhead Books. 2005.

Figley, Charles R., and Nash, William P. (Eds.), Combat Stress Injury: Theory, Research, and Management. New York: Routledge, 2007.

Jones, James. *WWII.* New York: Grossett and Dunlap, 1975.

Kopelman, Jay and Melinda Roth. *From Baghdad, With Love.* Connecticut: Lyon Press, 2006.

Levine, Mark L. *Rescuing Sprite: A Dog Lover's Story of Joy and Anguish.* New York: Pocket Books, 2007.

Luttrell, Marcus and Patrick Robinson. *Lone Survivor.* New York: Little, Brown and Company, 2007.

McConnell, Patricia B. *For the Love of a Dog: Understanding Emotion in You and Your Best Friend.* New York: Ballantine Books, 2006.

Sturkey, Marion F. *Warrior Culture of the U. S. Marines.* 2 ed. Plum Branch, SC: Heritage Press International, 2003.

Swofford, Anthony. *Jarhead.* New York: Scribner, 2003.

Underwood, Lamar, ed. *The Quotable Soldier.* Connecticut: Lyon Press, 2005.

United States Marine Corps. *United States Marine Guidebook of Essential Subjects.* Washington, DC: Marine Corps Institute, 1983.

Williams, Kayla. *Love My Rifle More Than You: Young and Female in the U.S. Army.* New York: W. W. Norton & Company, 2005.

PHOTO CREDITS